Today's Business Communication

Today's Business Communication

A How-to Guide for the Modern Professional

Jason L. Snyder and Robert Forbus

Today's Business Communication: A How-to Guide for the Modern Professional
Copyright © Business Expert Press, LLC, 2014.

First published in 2014 by
Business Expert Press, LLC
222 East 46th Street, New York, NY 10017
www.businessexpertpress.com

ISBN-13: 978-1-60649-672-5 (paperback)
ISBN-13: 978-1-60649-673-2 (e-book)

Business Expert Press Corporate Communication Collection

Collection ISSN: 2156-8162 (print)
Collection ISSN: 2156-8170 (electronic)

Cover and interior design by Exeter Premedia Services Private Ltd., Chennai, India

First edition: 2014

10 9 8 7 6 5 4 3 2 1

Printed in the United States of America.

Abstract

This handy guide to excellent business communications is perfect for both college students and business professionals. Whether preparing for a career, launching a career, or advancing in a career, the savvy professional understands that every organization expects employees to be exceptional business communicators. *Today's Business Communication: A How-to Guide for the Modern Professional* leads readers through the most frequently encountered business communication situations. Two business partners who are also business school professors share their combined 30 years of marketing and communication experience with readers in this accessible, entertaining, and informative guide. The authors enhance the readers' experience through anecdotes from business professionals from different industries.

Keywords

business communication, managerial communication, communication, business writing, business reports, business letters, public speaking, presentations

Contents

Foreword

We promise we won't tell you that everything you are doing right now is wrong. We promise that we won't harp on every fine point of grammar and syntax. Instead, we promise to use every tool at our disposal to inspire you to be a better business communicator. If you don't want to be better, this book can't help you. But, if you want to improve, or if you realize that you need to improve, we're the right coaches for you and this is the right playbook to help you succeed. In fact, you should be able to read this playbook while on a cross-country flight and put its advice to use by the time you hit the ground, if not sooner. Just like coaches and their teams work hard, follow their playbooks, and have fun while playing their games, you should also expect to work hard and have a little bit of fun playing the business communications game.

CHAPTER 1

Why Must I Read This Book and Follow Your Advice (or Else)?

When you read this chapter's title you may have thought, "Who do these guys think they are?" If so, relax. We're not nearly as full of ourselves as the chapter title suggests. Just like the late, life-and-success coach Dale Carnegie, we sincerely believe the following: "People rarely succeed unless they have fun in what they are doing."[1] Our assumption, and forgive us if we are assuming incorrectly, is that you want to be successful in your career. We also assume you want to have fun along the way. After all, if your work is fun, it's a lot less like work and a lot more like play.

This entire chapter is devoted to helping you gain a light-hearted perspective on how you can achieve success as a business communicator, and we are determined to have at least a little bit of fun along the way. So, why are we approaching our book in this manner? Let us answer that question by telling you a secret about ourselves. *We have read a lot of wicked-dull books.* It's true. Between the two of us, we have two doctoral degrees, three master's degrees, two bachelor's degrees, and nearly 40 years of combined business and communications experience. Believe us when we tell you we know how dull many textbooks are. While it's okay with us if you do not find our book to be a laugh riot, we hope you at least find it more interesting than many books you have read previously.

And speaking of fun, game show host Ryan Kristafer knows a thing or two about the relationship between success and fun. At the time of writing, Ryan is 22 years old; already, he has earned a degree in business, launched a career as an Internet entrepreneur (*LIVE game guy*), and is the top emcee/host at the sec-ond largest casino in the United States. Ryan says that half of what he does is building relationships and increasing his networks. He explains that the key to good relationships and networks in business is remembering that the people you meet today may not be immediately important to your business, but could become very important 5 years or more in the future. He also says relationships and networks must have mutual benefit—the benefit can't be a one-way street.[2] Ryan also offers advice on public speaking. You can find him on YouTube.

Communication Is About Relationships

Many, if not most, communication books focus on the process model.[3] To demonstrate how the process model works, we'll use an example from CBS television's *The Big Bang Theory*, which was, according to the Neilson Company, the #1 show in the valuable 18–49 demographic for the week ending February 13, 2013. Let's imagine that "Penny" is sitting on "Leonard's" couch. She thinks about what she wants to say and then speaks those thoughts to him. He responds to her with some hilarious facial expression and says something back to her that makes the audience laugh. *The Big Bang Theory* scenario just described is an example of what researchers call encoding a message through symbolic and spontaneous messages.[4,5]

Although the process model helps us to understand barriers to effective communication—for example, how "Sheldon" grinding away on a blender in the kitchen behind "Penny" and "Leonard" could present interference, thus preventing "Penny's" message from being accurately delivered to "Leonard"—it does not get to the real heart of communication: relationships. Part of what makes the comedy in *The Big Bang Theory* so hilarious to audiences is the complicated and dysfunctional relationships shared among the characters on the show.

Without communication, relationships of any kind would fail to exist. And just like the characters on *The Big Bang Theory*, we have in both our personal lives and our business careers, complicated, sometimes humorous, relationships with our coworkers, supervisors, direct reports, vendors, clients, customers, and stockholders, among others.

Great business communicators—and you should start lumping yourself into that category—must think beyond the process and understand that business communication is all about business relationships.

This approach allows us to avoid dehumanizing our audiences, acknowledge the important role of relationships in our professional lives, and understand the interdependence and mutual influence that truly characterize our dealings with others.[6] When you think about the great communicators in your life, do you admire their ability to overcome audience members' psychological distractions or their ability to manage their relationships effectively?

Each Communication Carries Both Content and Relational Meanings

In their landmark book on communication and system principles, Paul Watzlawick, Janet Beavin, and Don Jackson presented five basic rules about communication.[7] Although all five rules are worthy of your understanding, the second has practical usefulness for great business communicators: *You communicate both content and relationship information in every message.* What this rule is telling you is that not only are you giving a greeting when you say "good morning" to a customer, you are also sending information about the relationship between you and the customer. For example, the barista at Starbucks is greeting you, and at the same time letting you know that you are a needed, valued, welcome presence in the store. Part of the relational information the barista is communicating to you at Starbucks is that you have the power in the relationship.[8] After all, the customer is always right, right?

Watzlawick, Beavin, and Jackson's Five Communication Rules Paraphrased

1. You can't communicate by yourself.
2. You communicate both content and relationship information in every message.
3. You and your communication partners organize messages with verbal "punctuation" that is similar to punctuation in written messages.
4. You communicate verbally and nonverbally.
5. Your communication with others is influenced by the nature of the relationship you have with those people.

Nonverbal Matters

For decades, people in popular culture have repeated the belief that non-verbal communication is 12.5 times more powerful than verbal communication. This belief rests in the psychological research of Albert Mehrabian.[9] Without getting into a complicated debate over research methods, let's just say that popular culture may have applied Mehrabian's research a bit too broadly. However, we agree with the conventional wisdom that non-verbal communication is important. The best business communicators understand that reading and sending nonverbal communication is an art that can be practiced to advantage in dealing with others.

Let's return to Starbucks and our barista example from before. We established previously that part of the barista's "good morning" greeting was sending you relational message information. Much of that information being communicated by our barista is nonverbal (see rule 4). Examples of this nonverbal communication include his smile, the warmth of the expression in his eyes, the openness in his body language, or perhaps the slight inclination of his head toward you.

We're spending time refreshing your memory about nonverbal communication because too frequently in business communication we forget that business is not entirely rational. Our organizations are filled with people, people who have emotions. For example, one of us once had a friend who complained that although he and his supervisor shared a cubicle, the supervisor would communicate even simple messages by email. In this case, the supervisor's content was reaching its intended recipient. To the friend, however, the message really being sent was "I don't like you enough to turn around and speak to you." Was that the supervisor's intent? Maybe not, but when we don't pay attention to both the content and relational meanings of our messages, our communication effectiveness declines. Great communicators do the hard work of making sure that they attend to both meanings.

Nonverbal Communication Complements Verbal Messages

Your nonverbal communication should complement or reinforce your verbal messages. Effective business communicators understand this principle very well. What they understand is that when our verbal communication and nonverbal communication do not match (e.g., telling a prospective employer how interested you are in a job while leaning back, rolling your eyes, and crossing your arms), audiences give greater weight to the nonverbal behavior. So, when our verbal communication and nonverbal communication do not match, our messages lose clarity and become open to interpretation. And if there is one thing business communicators don't like, it is losing control of their messages.

Think about a time when you suspected that a coworker was being dishonest with you. Chances are that, once your suspicion was adequately aroused, you began to pay attention to the coworker's nonverbal behavior (e.g., failure to make eye contact, taking longer to respond to questions). Our interpretation of those behaviors was likely influenced by our past experiences with the person, with other persons, and by other outside factors. Although that approach is natural and reasonable, studies suggest those nonverbal behaviors are not the most indicative of deception[10] and that we are not very good lie detectors.[11] Therefore, when our coworker's words are not matched by adequate eye contact, we tend to presume deception. Unfortunately, that conclusion may very well be incorrect. To ensure our messages are perceived appropriately, we must work to make sure that our verbal communication and nonverbal communication do not contradict one another.

It is probably worth mentioning that little white lies can be useful when used to help others avoid embarrassment. For example, when your pregnant spouse complains of feeling fat, it might be useful to tell her she has never looked more beautiful. Or, if your new colleague comes to a meeting in mismatched socks, and asks whether anyone has noticed, you might tell him that he looks epic.

Your Written Messages Are Permanent

Despite advances in social media, email is still one of the primary communication tools in the workplace.[12] Although we use it frequently each day, too many communicators forget that email can often carry the same legal weight as other forms of written communication. In the section that follows, we share advice from an attorney who explains how companies and their employees can find themselves in big trouble because of emails. Too many of us forget that the things we put in writing have a way of becoming permanent. To the contrary, great communicators are thoughtful about those things they choose to put in writing.

Although there are a number of examples of inappropriate or embarrassing written communications "going viral," the case of former CIA Director David Petraeus is particularly chilling. Why? Because Mr. Petraeus, a former U.S. military general, resigned in disgrace from his position reportedly because of an inquiry linking him to an extramarital affair with his biographer, Paula Broadwell. The investigation was reportedly launched because social planner Jill Kelley began receiving harassing emails that were traced to Ms. Broadwell.[13] As part of that investigation, the FBI found another email account that was shared by Mr. Petraeus and Ms. Broadwell in which they left messages for one another in draft messages (i.e., without actually sending the messages). As a result of the revealed affair, Mr. Petraeus's reputation was destroyed, and his career was over.[14]

The Petraeus example is enlightening because it is easy to think about the workplace bully who sends threatening emails. But, the retired general is a bright and accomplished individual. He served in the military for nearly three decades, reached the highest echelons of the intelligence community, and holds a PhD degree from Princeton. He used a clever plan to keep his communications with Ms. Broadwell clandestine. Yet, despite his best efforts, his written communications, his emails, proved to be his undoing.

Busy People, Emails, and Communications Overload

Attorney Mary A. Gambardella is an expert on email. In fact, during a 2013 presentation, she told her audience that email has become her favorite topic as a litigator, because for better or worse, email has replaced a lot of human contact, and email often has expensive, negative consequences. As a business communicator, you will need to remember that your workplace email messages can linger, even after deleted, for many years.

For example, Ms. Gambardella says she has employed forensic computer experts who were able to retrieve inappropriate emails that employees had *deleted* as far back as 2006. Wow. First, think about all of the emails you've sent this year. Now imagine all the emails you've written since 2006. Would each one pass legal scrutiny in a court of law? Probably not. But in business they really need to be able to pass such close consideration. Ms. Gambardella's advice on the matter: train your mind to think first, before writing a single line of a single email.

During her remarks, Ms. Gambardella also advised her audience to have company policies regarding email use and, if you're a manager, make sure those policies are implemented and monitored; and, if your employees violate your email policies, you, as a manager, must enforce appropriate penalties. Better to take disciplinary action against the policy violators than to engage expensive legal services to defend yourself and your firm against a lawsuit.[15]

Think about whether that email you're about to send is really necessary. Each day, new M.B.A. hires exchange approximately 200 email messages.[16] The average worker spends 650 hours writing more than 41,000 words in emails each year.[17] In addition, the average worker attends 62 meetings per month.[18] And sometimes we check email while attending meetings. We multitask despite the negative effects on our productivity.[19] Put simply, we are busy.

Time and Time Again

We are all bombarded by emails begging for our attention. As a result, we aren't able to pay attention to everything, either because there aren't enough hours in the day or we don't have enough interest to stay fully engaged. Therefore, the reality is that some emails get buried in our inboxes, while we delete or ignore others because either the sender or the subject line doesn't pass a cursory "so what?" test.

Although fewer people wear wristwatches today than in the recent past, because we rely on smartphones for the time, why don't you try to imagine you are wearing a watch? Next, pretend that the watch has been making a loud ticking sound all day. You probably have not—if you are lucky—noticed every loud tick that your watch has sent to your brain. Why not? Well, to get through the day, we pay more attention to things that matter to us.

Business communications—emails, voicemails, letters, memos, advertisements, and so on—similarly impinge on our senses like that imaginary ticking watch; and consequently, it is up to us to make sure that our messages get our audiences' attention and are not a waste of time. The trendy new Google glasses are a cool invention, and the high price will probably decline over time, but imagine all the additional messages we'll receive if we get a pair of those Google goggles. While we're thinking about this new wearable technology, we might also consider how we can use it as a means for creating trendsetting business communications.

Great business communicators know they have to make choices: (a) find a way to make messages stand out or (b) risk having communications become the imaginary ticking wristwatch that you are wearing. Great communicators understand that because people are busy, their time is precious and valuable. Being late for meetings, inviting people to meetings who do not need to attend, and holding individuals longer than scheduled are all sins to the great business communicators.

Clear and concise communication also plays a role in respecting people's time. As professors, we know that the vast majority of our students will never share our passion for communication and marketing. As a result of our passion, it can be difficult to keep our comments concise. But great communicators know that people's ability to maintain focused attention is rather limited.

Your Audience May Not Share Your Perspective

We often have a difficult time coming to terms with the reality that people don't always share our views. As we said before, the ideas we are passionate about are not necessarily the ideas others are passionate about. Even if others are passionate about the same ideas as we are, it does not mean they see or think about the idea in the same way. To test this notion, try playing the following game.

Ask a group of people to think of some common object, like ice cream, for example. Ask each person in the group to write down the first 10 things that come to mind when thinking about ice cream.

Compare all the lists and you will quickly discover that no two lists are exactly alike. Great business communicators know that if people don't think about ice cream the same way, then there is little hope that people will think about complex business processes or problems similarly. The business communications *trick* is to first understand how your audience thinks about your ideas. Then, write or speak about those ideas from their perspective.

When great communicators take the time to understand their audiences—what motivates them, what they know, what they care about—they can craft their messages to answer the *WIIFY* question. *WIIFY* stands for "What's In It For You?" Great communicators know that when they can answer the *WIIFY* question for their audience, they have greatly improved their odds of communication success.

Frederick Ferguson is an information technology (IT) consultant currently living and working in Canada. Born in the United States and educated in the United Kingdom, he has worked on six different continents for some of the biggest names in IT. Because his work is highly technical, and it can contribute to companies' success or failure, he understands that clear, effective business communication that considers the audience's perspective impacts companies' bottom lines. Frederick explained:

> In my space, which is data warehousing and information management, the subjects tend to be even more abstract than computer science in general. I struggle all the time to get my team to communicate to clients very complex ideas in a succinct and effective manner. That way, critical business decisions can be made with a clear understanding of the implications of those decisions. Effective communication helps stakeholders understand the trade-offs of their decisions, while collaboration and outcomes improve.[20]

The Myth of "Communication Breakdown"

Great communicators understand that although barriers to communication effectiveness exist, that communication breakdown is as real as Santa Claus, Snow White, or Bart Simpson. Communication breakdown is a myth. This myth allows people to deflect blame from themselves, the source of the communication failure, to the so-called communication breakdown. Great communicators know that with some hard work, they can overcome many communication barriers. Great communicators suffer communication failures, just like the believers in the great myth of communication breakdown. However, great communicators take responsibility for their communication failures, learn the appropriate lessons, and improve, all the while working hard to never repeat the same mistakes.

Your Credibility Drives Your Effectiveness

Great business communicators understand the importance of their credibility to their ability to communicate effectively. Your credibility comprises people's perceptions of your trustworthiness and expertise. In other words, people find you credible to the extent that they can take you at your word and believe that you have the knowledge or experience to write or speak on a given topic. In fact, credibility is one of the best predictors of people's attitudes toward you.[21] Moreover, credible sources are more persuasive than less credible sources.[22]

It's no surprise that the people others trust and believe to be experts are also more influential. Great business communicators work hard to maintain their credibility by delivering on their promises and offering educated opinions. They also know that losing one's credibility can have devastating professional consequences. Although the Petraeus story teaches us about this principle as well, we will share another example.

In October 2011, the northeastern United States was struck by a massive snowstorm that left more than 3 million people without electricity for up to 11 days. In Connecticut, more than 80,000 customers of Connecticut Light and Power (CL&P) were without power at some point during the 11 days of outages. During the immediate storm response, the Governor stood next to CL&P President and Chief Operating Officer, Jeff Butler, as he made promises about power restoration. A report by an outside agency later reported that as the days dragged on, customers became increasingly frustrated by the situation and the failure of CL&P to fulfill the promises made by Mr. Butler. The report concluded that CL&P— with Mr. Butler as the public face—developed restoration goals that they knew they would not likely reach. The company then announced these goals publicly.[23] After the first few days of storm response, the Governor stopped standing next to Mr. Butler during those press conferences and chose to leave the room while Mr. Butler addressed the media. CL&P and Mr. Butler suffered severe damage to their credibility. By mid-November, Mr. Butler resigned.

You Are the Message

Impression management is important to business success. Great communicators care for their reputation the same way companies protect their brands. Those who protect their reputation reap a number of workplace benefits. For example, research indicates that impression management is associated with supervisor ratings of one's likability, job performance, and citizenship behaviors.[24] In forming opinions about you, people will use whatever information they have available to them. This may not seem fair, but it is true.

Great communicators know that failing to understand this principle can be disastrous to one's reputation and career. Cyclist Lance Armstrong has admitted recently to using performance-enhancing drugs while he dominated the sport, despite denying it for many years. Not only had Mr. Armstrong denied allegations of "doping" for years, but he used the legal system to silence his critics. In fact, many people were upset more by the tone of his denials than by the nature of the lies they contained. In an article on the topic, National Public Radio's Linda Holmes summed up the public's feelings about the Armstrong denials:

> It's not just the offense that's offensive, and it's not even just the lying about the offense. It's the co-opting of the language of innocence. It's one thing to do something you shouldn't do; it's another thing to ape the gestures and the language and the rage that people feel when something really isn't true. To lie straightforwardly is just dishonest; to thunder about your innocence when you are guilty is to exploit your audience's darkest fears of being wrongly accused.[25]

As a result of his lies and self-righteous indignation, Mr. Armstrong's personal brand has been tarnished to the extent that even though he admitted to doping during a TV interview, the anti-doping agency won't consider reducing his punishment unless he admits to doping while under oath.

Can you ever imagine reaching a point where even when you admit to wrongdoing, people are unwilling to take your word for it? Great communicators understand that you are the message. What you say and what you do tell people something about you.

Conclusion

This chapter poses the question *Why Must I read this book and follow your advice (or else)?* After having read this chapter and its anecdotes that illustrate our points, we figure you have your own answer to the question. But, in case you need a little coaching on your answer, here are four possible responses to the question:

1. Great business communicators can avoid tragic, career-ending mistakes.
2. Great business communicators get ahead in their careers faster than poor business communicators.
3. Great business communicators understand people and their motivations and use their knowledge and understanding to accomplish career goals and advance companies' successful attainment of business goals.
4. All of the above.

CHAPTER 2

Why Must I Remember That Nothing on the Internet Ever Goes Away Completely?

You'll remember from Chapter 1 that there are many high-profile professionals who have written things that got them into trouble—media scandals, integrity losses, job losses, and so forth. You can imagine those people would really like to travel back in time and not hit the send key on those emails. And even when we delete messages that we don't want the world to see, people like Attorney Gambardella can hire IT forensics experts to find them. Nathan Cutteridge, who is an IT specialist in the financial services industry, explains that the latest version of Microsoft Exchange, a mail server product commonly used by businesses and institutions around the world, never really "forgets" anything. Just because you delete it from your machine, the electronic file remains on the server.[1]

Can you imagine the nightmare of having an inappropriate joke, a rant against a coworker, a NSFW (not suitable for work) jpeg, or a snide comment about a supervisor being forever retrievable? Tanked careers and sued companies and individuals would be the tip of the iceberg in such a situation. The easiest thing to do is to simply write an email and let it sit for a while in draft stage before sending. However, even drafts need to be business appropriate in language and content. The Petraeus case reminds us that deleted drafts can live on in Microsoft Exchange and other server-based email systems. And, caution your friends and relatives against sending you jokes to your workplace. The United States is a particularly sue-happy country, and many people may be offended by the things that you or I might just laugh off as not bothersome.

Writing Email

Although we have many different communication channels to use at work, email receives disproportionately heavy use.[2,3] In fact, the *Harvard Business Review* reported on a 2012 survey of 2,600 workers in the United States, United Kingdom, and South Africa who use email daily. What the survey demonstrated is that 76% of the survey respondents are exchanging documents, 69% are sending information to groups of people, 61% believe they are improving communication across time zones, 60% are using email as an accountability tool, and 59% use email to search for information. Any single one of those uses could expose you or your company to legal difficulties. Send the wrong document to the wrong person, and you've violated confidentiality. If you're in contract negotiations, for example, you could inadvertently share trade secrets that could get you fired. Yet, the *Harvard Business Review* said of email that it remains the "mule of the information age—stubborn and strong."[4]

Whether it is a metaphorical thoroughbred horse or a lowly plow mule, email is popular with both companies and employees. Email's popularity derives, in part, from corporate cultures that value the communications channel. It is also liked for its immediacy and accessibility. Email has been adopted by people from all four of the generational cohorts currently represented in the workforce: The Silents, The Baby Boomers, The Gen Xers, and The Millennials. According to the Pew Internet and American Life Project, all four groups reported email usage rates of 90% or greater![5]

In the first chapter, we told you that research suggests workers create 40,000 words across 200 emails in a year, which would be the equivalent number of words found in a 200-page novel. That fact suggests workers are quite prolific with their email production. Therefore, don't you think it's important to follow some best practices to make the most of your email "novel?"

When sending business email, please remember that readers and courts often give business emails the same legal weight as paper documents. If you put something in writing, you and your organization may be held liable. You should also remember that email is lean. This means that because the reader can only draw conclusions from text alone, the reader is more likely to draw inappropriate conclusions unless the writer takes special care to be clear. Here's a piece of advice: practice the A.B.C. of business writing, which means; if you do so, you'll be accurate, brief, and clear.

Emotional intelligence expert Daniel Goleman believes we have a negativity bias in the way we perceive email.[6] That bias causes us to assume that email content is negative in tone, when in reality it has a neutral tone![7] Think back, have you ever gotten an email or sent an email that was misinterpreted? We have. And we know how to avoid those mistakes *most* of the time. Although email is easy to use, you still want to be both conversational and professional in your writing style. Here are some tips to get the most from your email experience.

Tips for Composing Emails

Compose Messages Offline

This approach gives you the time to make sure you really want to send that message.

Write Short, Actionable Subject Lines

For example, use two action words describing the audience's desired action and follow those words with a description of the topic. Recently, one of the book's authors (Jason) had to receive an answer to a question about an accreditation report he was writing for a busy executive-level university administrator. In that case, he used the subject "Please Advise – Accreditation Report Question." The busy administrator responded from her smartphone within an hour (unbelievably fast in the world of academia)!

Use Courteous Greetings and Sign-Offs

Just because the channel is easy to use and allows you to send messages quickly, it is no reason to be curt or rude. For individuals above you in the organization, begin your email with Dear Mr./Ms. ___ (last name). For individuals who are at your same level or below in the organization, you can begin your email with Dear ____(first name). Likewise, adopt a standard closing for all your emails. "Sincerely," "sincerely yours," "best regards," "warm regards," and "many thanks" are examples of email closings, or sign-offs, that we see in professionals' emails. Also, set up a signature line for every email you send that gives your name, your job title, the name of your company/organization, the mailing address, and your phone number. Some will also include a website address in the signature line. This little trick ensures that people receiving your emails can always get back to you using the communications channel of his or her preference.

Use the Top-of-Screen Test

If you're like most people, your workplace uses a program such as Microsoft Outlook as its email client. This tool does so much more than send and receive email; it holds your calendar, makes appointments, provides a to-do list, among other things. As a result, the emails you read may take up only half of the screen. It is in these few lines that people determine whether to take action on a message or bounce to the next one. Make sure the most important information or request appears in the top-half of the screen. If it is buried near the end of the message, your reader may not even look at it. Simply put, place the "ask" at the beginning, not the end.

Use Bulleted and Numbered Lists

Another way to make important pieces of information stand out in an email is to offset it in a bulleted or numbered list. Use lists only for important pieces of information. Remember the following rule about lists: *if everything is important, then nothing is important.* Do not make bullets or numbered lists if you have fewer than three points.

Don't Send Anything That You Wouldn't Want to See Published

This advice continues to be good; just ask Arthur Samberg. If you don't know Mr. Samberg, Google him. Gail Lavielle is a friend and colleague of ours who was an international public relations (PR) executive on two different continents and recently turned her considerable talents and skills to a career in government service as a member of the General Assembly. Her good advice for writing, behaving, and speaking: "Nothing in life will take you farther than graciousness." If you don't have a good handle on what graciousness means, Google it. It will take you far. Finally, before sending an email, ask yourself whether you'd be comfortable seeing it published on the front page of *USA Today*, the *New York Times*, *Washington Post*, the *Miami Herald*, or worse still have it go viral online thanks to someone like Perez Hilton. If you have any concern about seeing the message published, with your name attached, revise, revise, and revise before hitting send.

Pick Unique Times to Send Messages, When Possible

Remember from Chapter 1 the principle that people are busy? Well, we all receive a deluge of emails during the business day. If you want to increase the odds that people attend to your messages, send them during off-peak hours. Think about a time when you might send the message and have it appear at the top of the receiver's inbox—like sending it at 8:30 a.m. if the person arrives at work at 9 a.m.

Don't Hide Behind Your Email

Sometimes you have to get out and see people. Effective communicators know that communication is about relationships. Email is not an effective method of developing relationships for all age groups or in all situations. Verbal and vocal cues are absent from asynchronous communication (such as email and voicemail), thus making relationship development less easy, particularly cross-generationally. There are times when speaking with a person directly will enhance, or at least minimize damage to, a working relationship. Email is inappropriate when you need to consider others' feelings, when you are angry, or when you need to make sure you are understood.[8] Think before hitting send. Oh, right, we've told you that before. Well, it bears repeating: Think before hitting send.

Pay as much Attention to Tone, Grammar, Punctuation, and Spelling as You Would in a Letter or Memo

Since the messages you write carry the same legal weight as printed, signed letters or memos, you should follow the same rules. Have you heard of the million-dollar comma? National Public Radio ran a fascinating piece on its *All Things Considered* program about the legal case between Rogers Communications and Bell Aliant over Rogers' use of Aliant's telephone poles. Rogers believed their contract was good for 5 years, and Aliant said the placement of the second comma in the following clause allowed it to terminate the contract before 5 years and save $2 million (Canadian):

> This agreement shall be effective from the date it is made and shall continue in force for a period of five (5) years from the date it is made, and thereafter for successive five (5) year terms, unless and until terminated by one year prior notice in writing by either party.

The court agreed with Aliant. So if your email carries the same weight as other documents, don't you want to make sure you aren't responsible for the next million-dollar comma?[9]

Avoid Overusing "cc" and "bcc"

People rightfully complain about being included unnecessarily on long email chains. Effective communicators consider carefully the recipients of their messages. Further, first-rate business communicators will often take the time to remove chains of email to get down to the most important piece of information before forwarding an email received from someone else, or multiple people. One of us (Robert), automatically hits delete on any messages that come from a particular colleague who lives in another part of the world. All those deleted messages were chains the colleague sent to scads of people with whom he wanted to share the joke or the political statement, or whatever. Come on, you do it, don't you? Most of us do, so why wouldn't we expect others to do what we are doing?

Text Messaging

Although email, face-to-face conversations, group meetings, and phone conversations are preferred channels for workplace communication, there is little doubt that text messaging is becoming increasingly important.[10] In fact, the Pew Internet and American Life Project recently reported that

80% of all cell phone owners use their phones to send and receive texts. Further, the project concluded that texting is "nearly universal among young adults, ages 18–29." Therefore, texting is in many places, and soon will be nearly everywhere, a major mode of workplace communication.[11]

Many writers frame the issue of texting as one of generational differences. The takeaway message is usually, "texting is an unproductive activity performed by young employees." Given the heavy use of text messaging by almost all age cohorts, that message is becoming increasingly hollow. There are not many hard-and-fast rules about appropriate text messaging at work, but attorneys and IT professionals are developing policies all over the country, even as we write this book. Please consider these points:

First, know whether your company has a policy in place about text messaging. Are you allowed to send text messages while at work? Some companies restrict sending text messages—even from personal devices—during work because of liability issues. The company can be held liable if you drive, text, and *crash* during the course of your work.

Second, if you send a message that can be construed as creating a hostile work environment, your employer can be liable. Beyond liability, some employers believe that text messaging reduces your productivity and is distracting for other workers. Regardless of whether you are issued a company cell phone, you must know your company's policy about texting. If your company policy allows text messaging, here are a few tips to keep in mind.

- Pay more attention to the people you are with than to your device.
- Maintain a professional tone in messages and use whole words, not text shortcuts. For example type great, not "gr8." Particularly when you communicate inter generationally, your audience may not know all the same shortcuts that you know, "IOHO" (in our humble opinion).
- Understand your audience's technology proficiency (do you know if the person on the other end uses texts?) Some "Baby Boomers" and "The Silents" refuse to text, or find it difficult to text because of certain medical conditions, including arthritis. Additionally, they may not subscribe to

a texting plan and do not care to incur charges for receiving text messages. Alternatively, it's not appropriate to assume that just because someone is young, he or she is technologically proficient. All too often in our classrooms, we have encountered students who admit, some with pride and others with shame, that they are not "computer people" or that they don't text.

- Use text messaging when you don't want to distract others via conversations or when your conversation needs some privacy (not legal privacy but personal privacy). And, keep your device set to vibrate. Few things are more annoying in a business meeting than 10 people around a conference table with all their text and email alerts sounding out loud.
- Don't hide behind text messages (conversations about critical business matters should not be treated flippantly).
- Consider the nature of the relationship between you and your audience when sending messages.

Writing for Social Media

Social media can be powerful business communication tools. These platforms have emerged and evolved at tremendously fast speeds. We currently have available to us social media tools such as social networking (e.g., Facebook, LinkedIn), microblogs (e.g., Twitter), blogs, media sharing (e.g., Flickr), and forums, among others. The rules of engagement and etiquette for social media channels have evolved almost as quickly as the platforms. In this section, we will discuss social media use from two perspectives: Personal and Business. In both cases, the user's goals are similar: to strengthen the person's professional brand as well as the business brand, build community, develop relationships, and respond quickly to people and issues we care about.

Tips for Personal, Professional Social Media Use

Do you have a social media presence? As we are writing this book, Facebook has more than 1 billion users,[12] Twitter eclipsed 500 million users,[13] and 800 million unique users visit YouTube each month.[14] Because we figure you may be using YouTube as much or more than we are, we suggested in Chapter 1 that you look up Ryan Kristoffer on YouTube to watch his advice on making presentations. LinkedIn, which many of us view as the leading "professional" social media site, boasts more than 200 million members.[15]

Some professionals avoid using social media for a number of reasons. For example, one of this book's authors (Jason) has a friend who refuses to have any social media accounts because he is afraid of mixing his personal and professional lives. Other people avoid using social media because they don't see the value or don't want to give up any of their perceived privacy. The decision to use social media is personal, but good reasons to do so include the following:

- Building your professional reputation and brand
- Enhancing job searches
- Extending your professional network
- Strengthening your existing professional network
- Staying informed about major trends and issues in your industry
- Sharing your knowledge and expertise with others

Many of us are anxious about using social media, and some of us approach social media use far too casually. Just as in business writing, our goal is to strike a balance between being too casual and being too stodgy and dull. By following a few simple rules and keeping the principles of effective business communicators (see Chapter 1) in mind, you can have an enjoyable and rewarding social media experience. Here are those simple rules:

Remember That You Are the Message

Consider yourself a brand and think carefully about what your social media accounts say about your brand. Your brand is not just about the things you say but also about the image you present to the world. Pictures matter just as much as words. Recently, an Alabama-based news reporter learned this lesson the hard way. She was terminated without cause after posting a number of "confessions" to her personal blog. Although some of her confessions—such as stealing mail from the mail room and *maybe* putting it back—were probably written tongue-in-cheek, her employer wasn't amused. The reporter may gain 15 minutes of fame from this exposure, but in the long run, her brand will almost certainly be tarnished.[16] It may not be fair, but we never said that life and communication are fair.

Be Focused and Authentic

Consider the professional reasons you have for engaging in social networking, find your niche, and try to stick to it as closely as possible. What are the topics or issues on which you can provide unique insight? For instance, Garr Reynolds (a.k.a., The Presentation Zen) shares extensively through social networking (website, blog, Twitter) information that is almost exclusively about improving public speaking skills. In doing so, he remains authentic by combining his deep knowledge of public speaking with his other passions, including jazz and storytelling.

Consider Both Intended and Secondary Audiences

You never know who might see your social media content. One of our former students was recently disciplined for an inappropriate Tweet from a personal account. In the tweet, he suggested that his company's hiring of a new executive-level leader was a downgrade and shared a rumor about why the outgoing executive was let go. The tweet was eventually seen by his direct supervisors. Although the tweet may have been funny for his intended audience, his secondary audience was less amused.

Be a Giver, not Just a Taker

This tip comes straight from the world of traditional, "offline" networking. The best way to get value out of your network is to put value into the network. See yourself as a resource for others. In a recent blog post, Kevin Shigley, director of Global Talent Acquisition for The Coca-Cola Company, reminded job hunters of the importance of finding "ways to share your knowledge and expertise." You can do so through Tweets, status updates, blog entries. You can also do so by reposting information that might be useful for individuals in your network. Finally, you can join professional conversations in discussion threads like those hosted by individuals and organizations on LinkedIn.[17]

Business Uses of Social Media

Although the primary focus of this book is to provide you with advice for improving your personal communications at work, we would be remiss if we did not mention business uses of social media. Businesses are increasingly going social. According to University of Massachusetts-Dartmouth researchers, as of 2012, 28% of Fortune 500 companies had a corporate blog, 73% had a corporate Twitter account, 66% had a Facebook page, 62% had a YouTube channel, and 2% had a Pinterest account.[18] Why are businesses using social media?

Many businesses use social media as a means of sharing information, and not just about product sales. In 2013, the Securities Exchange Commission ruled that corporations can share material information with investors through social media.[19] Businesses also use social media to connect with consumers and drive sales. For instance, WalMart's Facebook-based CrowdSaver app offers a discounted product to consumers if enough people "like" the deal. Once the threshold of likes is reached, consumers can purchase the discounted product. In doing so, WalMart is connecting with consumers by giving them some sense of control. To be able to "like" a deal, one must first "like" WalMart, a move that allows WalMart news to be fed to one's Facebook news feed.[20] Southwest Airlines has gained notoriety for its *Nuts about Southwest* social media site. The site started as a blog, but has developed into an integrated site, featuring the blog, videos, podcasts, Twitter feed, and more. The airline uses *Nuts about Southwest* to understand its consumers and to create a sense of community. In fact, the site's "About" page reads, "We want to build a personal relationship between our Team and you, and we need your participation. Everyone is encouraged to join in, and you don't need to register to read, watch, or comment."[21]

Whatever the reason, most businesses have decided to use social media. And social media is not simply the domain of those "communication professionals." If you choose to avoid social media in your personal life, you may still be involved in social media in your professional life. So you can't be like the proverbial stork who simply buries its head in the sand to avoid bad news. If you look at Southwest Airline's social media site, you should notice that the contributors come from many parts of the company, not just marketing and communication. In order to be authentic, consumers increasingly want to hear directly from employees, not some message filtered and preapproved by the firm's communication and legal departments.

Conclusion

This chapter poses the question *Why Must I Remember that Nothing on the Internet Ever Goes Away Completely?* After having read this chapter and its anecdotes that illustrate our points, we figure you have your own answer to the question. But, in case you need a little coaching on your answer, here are three possible responses to the question.

1. Great business communicators understand that just because you can say something, doesn't mean you should.
2. Great business communicators use social media to manage their professional brands.
3. Great business communicators do not leave electronic and social media communications to the "communication professionals."

CHAPTER 3

Why Must I Put My Audience First?

One of the most difficult lessons for business communicators to master is putting the audience first. So much of business communication is strategic, which means we need people to change a belief, attitude, or behavior in order for our communication to be effective. To be successful, we have to think clearly about our audience and how they will react to our communication. In this chapter, we provide advice for achieving your communication goals while paying special attention to your audience. One of the components of putting your audience first is making sure you provide them with a *quality* product. Therefore, we provide you with substantial advice on how best to avoid writing mistakes. Remember that one of us used to work for a boss who refused to read beyond a single error in a letter. That boss probably isn't the only person in the business world who holds such high standards.

Be Mission Driven

Whenever you prepare a business message of any kind, ask yourself the following: Why am I preparing this message? If you can't answer that question clearly and succinctly, then you really must consider whether you should be preparing your message at all.

Business communication is strategic. You're always trying to (1) get your audience to understand your message, and (2) get your audience to respond appropriately to your message. To be effective, all business communications need to accomplish those two goals. After all, it's not enough for your manager to understand that you deserve a salary increase if he or she doesn't grant your request. In order to fulfill these two goals, you must first have an idea of what you want to say and what type of response you're looking for. In other words, consider your message's *raison d'être*. To be effective, your messages need to have a reason to exist—they need to have a *purpose*. Business communicators who take the time to articulate the purpose of important messages are less likely to make strategic and tactical errors.

We see a message's purpose as being comparable to a company's mission statement. Mission-driven companies have a clear social mission and they pursue profit and realize growth through those avenues that bolster the mission. Mission-driven companies don't just chase dollars. They don't pursue profit and growth at the expense of their mission's goals. In these companies, decision making is driven by the mission. If a particular action does not support the mission, it is not undertaken. Your message's purpose statement should help you to make the important strategic decisions you will face when crafting your message. Purpose statements should help you to make difficult choices, provide you with direction, and help you get to the point.

So, what is a purpose statement? A purpose statement is a declarative statement that identifies your intended audience and what you want that audience to know, do, or believe as a result of exposure to your message.

Before you fire off that next email, take a moment and see if you can write down the message's purpose statement in a declarative statement. The purpose statement should not be one or two words, but a complete statement. For instance, *budget* and *cutting the budget* are not purpose statements. A purpose statement looks more like this: *I must convince the regional manager to cut his budget by 10% for the next fiscal year or issue layoff notices to two employees.*

Consider More Detailed Objectives

In addition to your higher order purpose, you should consider the following four questions:

1. What is it that you *really* want to achieve with your message?
2. What organizational goals are fulfilled by your message?
3. How can your message support your brand identity?
4. What effect do you want your message to have on the relationships involved?[1]

> Dear Paul,
>
> Please submit to me your unit's plan for cutting 10% from next fiscal year's budget. Alternatively, you may lay off two members of your unit.
>
> Kristin

Figure 3.1 Email about 10% budget cut

These four questions matter. The first question is pragmatic and forces you to think deeply about what you want. The second question is political and may make your audience more receptive to the message. Ideas that are attached to bigger organizational goals are more likely to be successful. The third question is self-serving. The final question serves as a reminder that communication is about relationships.

Before we look at these four questions in greater detail, consider the email message in Figure 3.1. The email is brief and clear, and it also fulfills the purpose. It is, in fact, a good message. But is it truly effective? No. If you want to transform your messages from okay to truly powerful and effective, you need to consider the four questions we outlined above.

For instance, if you look at the purpose statement we crafted above concerning the 10% budget cut, a deeper consideration of the four questions may help us to craft a more effective message. Let's consider the four questions in relation to our purpose statement:

> ***What is it that you really want to achieve with your message?***
> In answering this question, you will find that you will make a handful of strategic and tactical decisions. How much autonomy do you plan to give the regional manager in making budget cuts? Where specifically in the budget would you like cuts to be made? Should the regional manager treat the request as confidential? When do you need the cuts? In what format do you want the cuts to be delivered? Are you open to suggestions that do not include budget cuts, layoffs, or both?
>
> ***What organizational goals are fulfilled by your message?*** If your message supports one or more organizational goal, it is a good idea to remind your audience about those goals.

How can your message support your brand identity? We discussed the importance of impression management in Chapter 1. You should have an idea of how you want others to see you. You should also have the self-awareness to understand how your audience will likely perceive you as a result of your communications. Work to make sure that your messages reflect a positive light onto you.

What effect do you want your message to have on the relationships involved? The message and how you deliver it will influence the relationships between you and your audience as well as other relationships. For instance, if the regional manager chooses to lay off two workers, your message has had an influence on those relationships.

Given these four questions, how would you evaluate the revised email in Figure 3.2? Please read the email before you move on to our take on the email in Figure 3.3.

The email in Figure 3.2 is much improved, but is it truly effective? No. Most people would probably say that this email is good, especially in light of the original version. But, you shouldn't aim for being good or merely okay; you should try to be an authentic and polished professional communicator. The email in Figure 3.2 lacks real empathy and is inauthentic. It does not directly address how profoundly tough the assignment will be, and it is also needlessly filled with management speak. Most books will give you a bad and a good version of its sample messages, but we don't see

---

Dear Paul,

As you know, the company has decided to pursue a strategy of lean management. In an effort to begin building toward our 5-year goal, I am asking you to do the hard work of finding new efficiencies within your unit. Because you have proposed creative solutions to problems in the past, and pursuing lean management will require creativity, I trust that you will be able to deliver ideas for cutting 10% from your unit's budget for the next fiscal year. You have the option of laying off two employees, but I know that is not what either of us wants at this time.

I understand that I'm asking a lot of you, and I am grateful for your willingness to accept this challenge to move us toward a promising future. Please prepare a plan and submit it to me by June 15. I am happy to offer you whatever assistance you need. If you have any questions, or need resources to complete the plan, please reach out to me.

Sincerely,
Kristin

Figure 3.2 Improved email about 10% budget cut

the world as being so black and white. So, consider a third version of the email, which we've provided for you in Figure 3.3.

Look back at the three sample messages that we just provided to you. It is our contention that the third message is good because it considers what we call the *Two Ps of Message Prep—Purpose and People*. Although we should approach our messages in a mission-driven manner, we can only be truly successful if we also place our audience—the people—front and center. In this book, we will share many failed messages that failed because the writer thought a great deal about accomplishing his or her goals and thought very little about other people.

To complicate matters, our messages may serve one organizational goal while undermining another goal, all while influencing multiple relationships. In these treacherous waters, taking the time to think about our purpose and people is sound advice.

Jeffrey Kotz, who you will meet again in Chapter 5, has experience working in marketing and research analytics. He shared with us a common problem that occurs in his line of work. Employees in analytics and client services work interdependently. Those employees in client services must get new business and make clients happy. Those employees in marketing and research analytics

---

Dear Paul,

Recently, our company's leadership team made critical decisions about our future that will present us with considerable challenges and some pain. The decision to pursue lean management strategy, which means that each unit needs to find new efficiencies, is one that will be difficult.

I understand that the task that I am asking you to undertake will be awfully hard. But, I have every confidence in your ability to be creative in accomplishing tough tasks. Please apply your creativity and talent to suggest a menu of options for us to cut 10% from your unit's budget for the next fiscal year. While the easy option would be for you to lay off two employees, I know that neither of us wants to lay off valuable staff.

This assignment will challenge you, and I understand that I'm asking a lot of you. Please let me know whether you can prepare and email a plan to me by June 15, or whether you feel you need additional time, and if so, how much. Feel free to come to my office to discuss your concerns.

Sincerely,
Kristin

Figure 3.3 An even better email about 10% budget cut

provide research and data analysis services for the clients, but these employees must also do their work efficiently and try to analyze data in a way that meets company standards. In an effort to make new clients happy, employees in client services will say yes to research requests that require those in analytics to break company standards. The promises to the client are often made in writing and the promises also support a company goal of attracting new business and making clients happy. However, this situation adversely influences the relationships between those in analytics and those in client services. These promises are resource intensive for analytics and they set a precedent that company standards can be broken. Employees in analytics know that they will come under increased management scrutiny for failing to meet an important organizational goal. As a result, Jeff tells us that relations between the two departments can be strained. We aren't arguing that company standards are more important than client satisfaction, but we are pointing out that blind pursuit of one goal without considering the communication landscape can often have other negative and unintended consequences.

In the sections that follow, we will share with you a number of ideas to improve your writing. These tips are not designed with only you in mind. We provide these tips not just because they will make you a better writer—and they will—but also because we know your audiences will appreciate your efforts to adopt these tips.

Tips for Achieving Conciseness

As we discussed in Chapter 1, most people in business are busy—too busy to read lengthy prose. So, one way that we can be more considerate of our audiences is to work at avoiding common writing errors that result in excessive wordiness.

Are you asking why conciseness matters? We wouldn't blame you if you read through this section and asked yourself if it is really worth your time to save a few words here or there. We believe your time will be an investment. Because the dominant business culture is low context, we put nearly everything in writing. All of that writing takes time to produce, resources to print or save, and time and energy to read. Our words require lots of resources. Conciseness not only shows consideration for your audience, it also makes business sense because it saves time and money. So, make a pact with yourself today that you will try to be more concise. And to help you, here are four tips that add brevity to your messages.

Replace Flabby Expressions

Like many Americans, our sentences could stand to be leaner. Flabby expressions are a core contributor to this problem.[2] A flabby expression simply uses too many words to express a simple idea. In Figure 3.4, you can find a handful of flabby expressions that we encounter on a regular basis. Be on the lookout for these flabby expressions and work to eliminate them from your writing!

Delete Unnecessary Lead-Ins

Unnecessary lead-ins include phrases at the beginning of a sentence that add nothing to the sentence. In many cases, you can simply delete the lead-in and keep the rest of the sentence intact. For example, a bad newsletter that one of the authors (Jason) received recently began, *"I am writing this letter to you to inform you that..."* One of the best tools that we can use to eliminate flabby expressions is to think about the message from our readers' perspective. In this case, Jason knew that what he was reading was a letter. Moreover, he knew that the letter was written by the sender because the sender's name was signed at the bottom of the page and was also on the letterhead. These facts render the phrase useless and eliminate 11 words. Not bad for looking at only one sentence. So, be more concise by taking lead-ins and leading them out of your sentences.

Flabby Expression...	Lean Expression...
Despite the fact that...	Although...
It is our opinion...	We believe...
Please feel free to...	Please...
Due to the fact that...	Because...
At some time in the near future...	Soon...

Figure 3.4 Commonly used flabby expressions

Delete It Is/There Are Starters

We tell our students that of all the ways they can introduce conciseness into their writing, this tip is the easiest to follow. Look at the first two words of your sentences. Those sentences beginning with "it is," "it was," "there is," or "there are" have at least two to many words. They can be deleted. The sentence may need some additional modification, but in many cases, that modification will include the elimination of a pronoun or relative pronoun. So, eliminating the it is/there are starter often results in saving at least three words.

Here's an example. One of the book's authors is a distance runner who routinely runs half and full marathons. He recently received an email from a race coordinator with instructions, including the following sentence:

"There are shuttle buses that will bring you to the start site."

We can delete the "there are" starter and the relative pronoun "that" in the process—voila! The revision results in a sentence with three fewer words.

"Shuttle buses will bring you to the start site."

Watch Out for Redundancies

Admittedly, this tip is the most difficult to follow because it requires you to know the definitions of the words you use. Redundancies include words that describe or define the obvious. For example, the expression "absolutely essential" is redundant. By definition, something or someone is either essential or nonessential. Therefore, there exists no such thing as "degrees of essentiality." Here are a few other redundancies: (a) old antiques, (b) rules and regulations, (c) final outcome, and (d) true facts.

Tips for Achieving Clarity

Achieving conciseness demonstrates respect for your audience and saves time and money. In writing, however, conciseness is of little use without clarity. Achieving clarity—in our writing, not in man's quest for meaning—is another means by which we can put our audience first. Here are some tips for achieving clarity.

Use Simple, Concrete Words

As writers, we want to avoid losing control over how our messages are interpreted. Clarity is essential (not absolutely essential). To be clear, we need to use words that our readers will understand and define those words that may be ambiguous, or subject to multiple interpretations. According to the National Center for Education Statistics, the average adult in the United States reads at a level somewhere between the 8th and 9th grade levels.[3] When in doubt about word usage, ask yourself what an 8th grade student would understand.

The 1990s one-hit wonder Haddaway asked: "What is love?" In business writing, it's the type of word we want to avoid, not because we're heartless, but because love is abstract. Abstract words have no direct connection to our five senses and are open to multiple interpretations. We want to replace abstract words in our messages when we can do so without "dumbing down" the message. Using concrete words is one way that we can be clearer. Concrete words speak to the five senses. For instance, 10 miles per hour is more concrete than fast. Fast is abstract because it is a relative term that can mean different things to different people.

Here's another example. When we advise clients about writing cover letters, we tell them to get rid of statements like, "Please contact me for an interview at your earliest convenience." Not only does a sentence like that show a lack of assertiveness, it also lacks clarity. Instead, we advise them to write things like "I would appreciate the opportunity to discuss my qualifications in an interview. I will follow up with your office on June 15 to make sure that you have received my materials. Perhaps we can make arrangements for an interview at that time."

Use Active Voice Sentences

You can write sentences that are either active or passive. Readers find active voice sentences to be clearer than passive voice sentences. Active voice sentences follow the actor–action pattern, in which the actor is identified early in the sentence and the action performed by the actor appears later in the sentence. Active voice sentences identify who or what the actor is and does. By contrast, passive voice sentences tend to obscure the actor's identity and are, therefore, considered to be more ambiguous than active voice sentences. For example, Reggae singer–songwriter Bob Marley wrote the following lyrics in active voice.

Active: I shot the sheriff.

We know the sentence is active because the actor (I) appears in the sentence before the action (shot). This sentence answers very clearly the question, Who did what? The same sentence written in passive voice would look like any of the following.

Passive 1: The sheriff was shot by me.
Passive 2: The sheriff was shot.

These sentences do not answer as clearly the question, Who did what? In fact, the second sentence does not identify the shooter at all. Also, you should notice how passive sentences place the emphasis on the object of the action (the sheriff) instead of the actor (I).

Can you think of times when you might prefer to use passive voice? If you are the defense attorney representing the shooter, you would probably prefer passive voice sentence number two. In that sentence, your client isn't even mentioned. So, although you should try to use active voice as much as possible, there are times when passive voice has its advantages. In fact, when you use passive voice sentences, you are not committing an error; you are making a stylistic choice. Choose wisely. Prefer active voice.

Write Short Sentences

As you can see in Figure 3.5, there are four types of sentences: simple, compound, complex, and compound-complex. Longer sentences are more difficult for readers to understand and increase the likelihood of committing one or more errors in grammar and mechanics. Therefore, your readers will appreciate your use of short, simple sentences.

Use simple sentences as frequently as possible without reducing your document's readability. For most adults, children's stories have low readability because they rely heavily on simple sentences. The other three sentence structures have their place. They can enhance a document's readability. They can make a more powerful point by combining two simple sentences that work better as one sentence. In fact, complex

---

Simple sentence—A sentence containing one noun and one predicate.
> *Example: Jacob processed the paperwork.*

Compound sentence—A sentence combining two or more independent clauses.
> *Example: Jacob processed the paperwork, and he filed it today.*

Complex sentence—A sentence combining one independent with one or more dependent clauses.
> *Example: Finishing after the deadline, Jacob processed the paperwork.*

Compound-complex sentence—A sentence combining two independent clauses with one or more dependent clauses.
> *Example: Jacob processed the paperwork, although after the deadline, but he filed it today.*

Figure 3.5 Four types of sentences

sentences can be used to deliver bad news. Compound, complex, and compound-complex sentences have multiple clauses. In compound sentences, both clauses have equal weight because they are both independent clauses—an independent clause could be a complete sentence. Complex sentences have two clauses, but one of those clauses is dependent. Dependent clauses would be sentence fragments if left all alone; they depend on other clauses to make a complete sentence. You can place bad news in a dependent clause of a complex sentence to reduce the impact of the bad news.[4]

The type of sentences you use is a matter of style. You have the freedom to use all of the different types of sentences. Our advice, however, is to prefer simple sentences and to use the other types of sentences strategically.

Use Mechanics to Your Advantage

If you want certain pieces of information to stand out, then use the mechanics available to you in your word processing program. Just as we recommended in Chapter 1, you can emphasize key ideas through the use of **bold**, *italic*, <u>underlined</u>, or ***<u>a combination</u>*** of font styles. In addition, you can use one or more of the following:

- Bulleted and enumerated lists
- Color

- Tables and figures
- ALL CAPS
- Headings and subheadings.

We offer one note of caution, however. Too much bold, too many italics, or too many underlined words will detract from readability. Think about the childhood story of the boy who cried wolf. He cried wolf so often that no one believed him when the wolf was truly there. The same thing works for using different font styles. Likewise, think about the person who writes emails in ALL CAPS. We call that "screaming." So, if you use ALL CAPS too often, your reader stops attaching importance to what you are calling attention to as being important.

Tips for Helping Others Remember Information

Organize Your Thoughts

Think about how you organize the information that you present to people. It is easier for readers to remember information that is organized appropriately.

Put Information Into Chunks

Readers have an easier time remembering small pieces of information. When you must present large volumes of information or long lists of information to readers, find natural ways to organize and chunk the information. Information that is chunked is easier for our readers to store in their short-term and long-term memory.[5] Your reader will thank you for it.

To drive home these points about information retention, you can play a little game that we play with our students. Ask a friend to look at the list of words in Figure 3.6. Give your friend 30 seconds to review the list and memorize the words. Take the list away at the end of 30 seconds. Before you let your friend tell you the words that he or she remembers, ask him or her an engaging question about another topic. For example, you can ask his or her opinion about a recent sporting event. After a very brief discussion, ask the friend to tell you all of the words that he or she remembers.

Boxer	Chrysler
Four	Beagle
Cheesesteak	Honda
BMW	Eight
Twelve	Volvo
Hot dog	Poodle
Lasagna	Twenty
Subaru	French fries
Cookie	Weimaraner
Schnauzer	Seventeen

Figure 3.6 *Twenty pieces of information*

Boxer	Hot dog	Chrysler	Eight
Schnauzer	Lasagna	Honda	Twelve
Weimaraner	Cheesesteak	Subaru	Twenty
Beagle	Cookie	BMW	Seventeen
Poodle	French fries	Volvo	Four

Figure 3.7 *Twenty pieces of information organized and chunked*

Now ask a second friend to review the list of words in Figure 3.7 contains the same 20 words found in Figure 3.6. Again, give the friend 30 seconds to review the list. Take the list away at the end of 30 seconds. Then, ask the friend an engaging question about another topic. After a very brief discussion, ask the second friend to tell you all of the words that he or she remembers.

Who performed better, the first or the second friend? We'll put our money on the second friend. When your friends see the two lists, the reason for the performance differential should be immediately obvious. Consider your audience by organizing and chunking information appropriately.

Avoiding Common Grammar and Writing Blunders

We have seen thousands of grammar and writing blunders. Although, as we will discuss in Chapter 4, nobody expects you to be perfect, you also don't want to have the reputation as the person who makes lots of mistakes. We believe, in fact, that some mistakes do more damage to your credibility than others. Below, we will provide you with a description of those errors. Before we do so, however, your best bet to avoid common grammar and writing blunders is to work constantly on your writing skills. If you want to improve your skills beyond those we offer, then you should consider using one or more of the resources in the following list.

Many colleges and universities have posted on their websites advice about how students can avoid getting on teachers' nerves with common writing mistakes. Instead of developing our own lists of advice for you, we have compiled a list of some great online resources that you should bookmark.

- George Mason University's advice on avoiding common grammar mistakes is helpful. http://classweb.gmu.edu/WAC/EnglishGuide/Critical/grammar.html
- Wisconsin University's Writing Center's advice on avoiding 12 common writing errors provides useful assistance. http://writing.wisc.edu/Handbook/CommonErrors.html
- Westminster College's list of avoidable mistakes is great for novice and intermediate writers. http://www.westminster.edu/staff/brennie/writerro.htm
- Purdue University's online writing lab with exercises can help you polish your command of English grammar and writing. http://owl.english.purdue.edu/exercises/

If the academic guides aren't for you, then we also recommend the Grammar Girl's blog, which can be found at http://grammar.quickanddirtytips.com/

We would be remiss if we did not recommend our favorite book on style, *The Elements of Style* by William Strunk, Jr. and E. B. White. You can pick up a copy of the book for less than $2 or you can find an edition online at http://www.crockford.com/wrrrld/style.html

And now, we present common grammar and writing blunders that can damage your credibility.

Possessives and Contractions

In reality, these are two different but related issues. They are related by the apostrophe. We may use apostrophes when using the possessive form of a noun and when writing a contraction. For example, in the phrase, *the cat's meow*, the word "cat's" is a possessive requiring an apostrophe. That is to

---

Use apostrophes for possessive nouns.
  Example: *Jason's marketing report*
Use apostrophe + s for possessive nouns that do not end in "s."
  Example: *Jason's marketing report*
Use an apostrophe—most of the time—when the possessive noun ends in "s."
  Example: *The consultants' marketing reports*
Use apostrophe + s for possessive nouns that end in "s" and can be pronounced after you add apostrophe + s.
  Example: *The boss's decision about the marketing reports*

Figure 3.8 *Guidelines for using apostrophes*

say, the cat possesses the meow. In the sentence, *don't run away from your writing problems*, the word "don't" is a contraction of the words "do" and "not." For most of us, that's the easy part, but possessives and contractions can be a little more complicated.

For instance, what's the difference between "your" and "you're?" The first is a possessive and the second is a contraction. In this case, the possessive does not require an apostrophe, but the contraction needs one. Similarly, many people use "its" and "it's" incorrectly. Again, the former is possessive and the latter is a contraction. An easy way to know if you're using "you're" and "it's" correctly is to replace the contraction with the words that the contraction represents. Then, say the sentence out loud. If "it is" or "you are" sounds wrong, then you probably need to use "its" and "your" instead. Figure 3.8 offers some additional guidelines for working with possessives.

Word Choice

Some words sound similar, have spellings that are almost the same, but have different meanings. Writers frequently make the incorrect selection in these situations. Here are some of the most common examples of these words that baffle many writers:

- There/Their/They're—They're is a contraction, their is a possessive, and there will work in all other cases.
- Affect/Effect—Affect is a verb, and effect is typically used as a noun.
- Then/Than—As a simple guide, you use than when making comparisons and then when you are not making comparisons.

- Are/Our—Our is a possessive, and are is a helping verb.
- Complement/Compliment—A complement is a nice addition to something, while a compliment is a nice thing you can say about someone else.
- Principal/Principle—A principal is a high-ranking individual or concept, and a principle refers to something that is fundamental.

Number Use

Business writers commonly misuse numbers. To help you use numbers correctly in most situations, here is some advice in three categories:

- General Use—(a) Write numbers one through ten as words, (b) write numbers 11 and above as figures, and (c) write numbers as words if they appear at the beginning of a sentence.
- Money and Dates—(a) Write sums greater than $1 as figures, (b) write numbers in dates as figures if the day appears after the month (e.g., June 10, 2013), and (c) write numbers in dates as ordinals if the day appears before the month (e.g., 10th of June).
- Clock Time—(a) Write numbers as figures when expressed with a.m. or p.m. (e.g., 5:30 p.m.), (b) drop the colon and last two digits when referring to the top of the hour (e.g., 5 p.m.), and (c) write numbers as words or figures when written with the word "o'clock" (e.g., five o'clock or 5 o'clock).

In addition to these guidelines, we urge you to aim for consistency. For instance, if you have a date and time in the same sentence, treat both in the same manner. Consider the following example: *Please attend the 4 o'clock meeting on July 15.* Although you have the option of writing "four" rather than "4," the latter is consistent with your use of "15."

Capitalization

The rules governing capitalization are easy to follow, but commonly misused. First, you should capitalize proper nouns (e.g., Connecticut).

You should also capitalize titles when they precede a person's name (e.g., Vice President Jenkins). You do not need to capitalize the title when it either follows a person's name (e.g., Trevin Jenkins, vice president of marketing) or is not associated with a person's name (e.g., the vice president of marketing).

Commas

Commas can be a real head-scratcher for even the most experienced writers. We hope these guidelines will help you in most situations:

- Add a comma after a person's name when followed by a degree (e.g., Robert Forbus, PhD).
- Add commas to set off elements that are not essential to the meaning of the sentence (e.g., Next Wednesday, the same day I go to the dentist, is the only afternoon that my calendar is clear).
- Add a comma after an introductory clause or phrase (e.g., When you're ready to meet, give me a call).
- Add commas when words are repeated (e.g., He was really, really hungry).
- Add a comma when two coordinate adjectives are used to describe a noun (e.g., His boss was an angry, little man).

Conclusion

In business communication, we have many opportunities to put our audience first. Having a clear purpose gives us the opportunity to target our communications to the appropriate audience while respecting the time and energy of those who do not need to receive our messages. Considering more detailed objectives as we craft our messages provides us with opportunities to demonstrate respect for our audiences and nurture our relationships with them.

Working to improve our writing's conciseness and clarity gives us the opportunity to demonstrate that we care about our audience's time.

Keeping in mind how audiences process and recall information grants us the opportunity to make sure our audiences hear and remember our messages. When we pay attention to the details, such as grammar and mechanics, we effectively manage the impressions the audience forms about us while also enhancing our clarity.

CHAPTER 4

Why Must I Remember That Communication Is About Relationships?

Judith Wegner Weir, an account coordinator at a PR firm, grew up in Germany and earned a degree at IBK Göttingen, a university in her home country. About 8 years ago, she moved to the United States, where she earned a business degree. Through her studies and her work, Judith has learned the importance of relationships. In a recent conversation with us, Judith said:

> Most of my work involves working with journalists to gain publicity for my clients. I write media advisories and news releases, and make follow-up calls to reporters at media outlets. Sometimes journalists can be unresponsive to contact from public relations practitioners. I have to build relationships with reporters, making sure I come across as credible, professional, warm, and friendly. I find that after I make initial contact with the reporters, and build a positive, professional relationship with them, they return my calls and emails. Another point that I make is to always respond to reporters' emails within 30 minutes of receiving them. That type of responsiveness is very important when building and then maintaining good relationships with colleagues. I also make the effort to learn what interests people when I'm trying to influence them. Relationships in the communications business are much easier to build when you focus on the needs of the other person, rather than your own.[1]

You probably have your own definition of the word "relationship," but because we are academics, we think we should define it for you, in order for you to share our understanding of the word. The online version of the *Oxford Dictionary* supplies the following definition of relationship, and we like it: "the way in which two or more concepts, objects, or people are connected, or the state of being connected; the way in which two or more people or organizations regard and behave toward each other."[2]

In Chapter 1, we discussed the differences between verbal and nonverbal communications. Now, we will turn our attention to the ways that both verbal and written communication can build positive relationships or destroy them. Consider, for example, Brooke Wilson's workplace experience:

I assumed I was entering a reasonably professional job, and I respected professionalism. However, when I got to my first day at my home branch, my assistant manager met me at the door, before the branch opened. She walked me to her office. She sat down at her desk, and I took the seat beside her. I expected her to show me around or begin to tell me how the day begins at the branch. Instead, she begins to tell me about my coworkers. She literally ran down the list of all my coworkers, their names, how long they had worked there, whether they were a good employee or not (according to her), and even volunteered personal information about them. In those first few moments, I realized this lady took the cake as far as being wrong in so many ways. I immediately developed an opinion of her that wasn't good. I later learned the supervisor had a similar talk with a coworker who had been hired about a year before me. Needless to say, I found it difficult to respect her or her position as supervisor. I worked at that job for more than 2 years and I can honestly say I hated it. It was hard to take orders from her and to take anything she said seriously because I didn't think much of her. She ruined her first impression with me from the beginning. I often wonder what she said about me to those coworkers who came in as new employees after me.[3]

Brooke survived her *yuck* job with the supervisor from Hades. She completed her business degree in 2013, after having returned to school full-time and working several years in retail and financial services. Today

1. Think before you speak or write. Consider the way in which your audience will receive your message.
2. Listen and ask questions. Demonstrate that you care about others.
3. Listen more than you talk. Show others that you know how to give and take in a communication exchange.
4. Avoid the blame game. Prove you're a professional by accepting responsibility for mistakes, rather than blaming others and making excuses.
5. Steer clear of "shoulds" and "should nots." Show your professionalism by suggesting what others *might consider* doing, rather than telling them what they *should do*.
6. Deploy positives rather than negatives. Encourage others by showing what they are doing well and how they can do even better, rather than focusing on what they're doing wrong.
7. Use "we" and "you" more than "me" or "I." Build credibility and likability by avoiding the quicksand of self-centeredness and self-aggrandizement.
8. Offer to help, rather than waiting to be asked. Maintain relationships by volunteering proactively to help out, suggesting resolutions to problems, or both, instead of hanging back until someone calls on you.
9. Avoid speaking negatively about others. Consider the array of possible types of professional relationships, personal relationships, or both, one individual may have with another.
10. Keep (negative) emotion in check. Short-term surrender to anger, frustration, annoyance, or hurt can easily derail your success and your professional future.

Figure 4.1 Ten tips to build positive professional relationships

she lives and works in South Florida. But Brooke's situation could have been very different if her supervisor had followed our 10 tips in Figure 4.1 to help you while communicating, whether orally or in writing.

When we ask you to remember that communications is about relationships, you can probably already see where we are leading you, especially considering Brooke's and Judith's stories and the 10 tips. To reiterate, relationships can be positive or negative, and as such the communications that accompany those relationships can be positive or negative. Consider the following two responses to a child's question about whether he or she can have dessert. Remember that the parent is trying to get the child to make healthful choices.

Parental Response #1: *No, unless you want a peach.*
Parental Response #2: *Yes, of course. We have some juicy, sweet peaches. Would you like me to get one of those for you?*

You can guess that the second response would be more likely to create excitement about peaches. Plus, it gives the child a sense of control over the situation because the parent encouragingly asks, rather than authoritatively dictates. The second response might even help the child to develop lifelong healthful eating habits and a more positive relationship with food.

Let's next consider a situation that you might encounter, or perhaps, may have already experienced. Let's say you've applied for a job that you really want, and you believe you had a terrific interview last week. A letter comes in today's mail, in an envelope with the name of the company where you hope to work. Here are two versions of the first two sentences of that letter:

Version #1. We regret to inform you that you will not be hired for the accounting position with Zimpal Group LLC. We will keep your résumé on file for 6 months, should another position for which you are better qualified becomes available.

Version #2. You were an outstanding candidate who performed well in your interview. An alternate candidate, however, one who has 2 years more accounting experience than you have, was the successful applicant for the position with Zimpal Group LLC.

Now, which letter would you rather receive? Which opening statement builds a more positive relationship? We hope you answered Version #2 because that version is shorter, less wordy, more professional, and demonstrates more thoughtfulness than Version #1. Notice, also, that the emphasis in the second version is upon the reader, not the sender, of the letter. The name of the company falls dead last in Version #2. The *"you"* focus in business communication is critical. Put yourself and the company in the background and put your reader, or listener if you are speaking, in the metaphorical front row.

Delivering Bad News

Often in business communication, we have to deliver bad news. It might be in a presentation to shareholders, in an interview with the media, in a letter to a customer, or even in a letter to a job candidate. Two of the best questions to ask yourself, when planning a communicative message of bad news are these: "How would I want to receive this message?" and "How would I want someone to deliver bad news to the person I love most?" Putting yourself into the role of the receiver of bad news is an exercise in empathy. Empathetic communications are highly effective when delivering bad news. Below you'll find an example.

Sample Response to Negative Customer Feedback

Zimpal Group, LLC
1028 Boulevard
Box 314
West Hartford, CT 06119
860.578.8643

January 31, 2014
Ms. Sheree Sherazod
1234 Maple ST
Made Up City, CT 12345-678

Dear Ms. Sherazod—

Thank you for your recent letter to us explaining your experience when you attended our seminar last month in Made Up City. Your correspondence demonstrated a need for Zimpal Group to review client registration processes at its seminars. Please accept our apologies for your negative experience with our registration desk. At Zimpal, we strive to exceed our clients' expectations, and clearly we were unable to do so with you.

Your interaction with our temporary employee at the registration desk was unfortunate. We are unable to refund the price of your attendance, because despite the unpleasant demeanor of the temporary employee, you chose to attend the full-day's session. You might be interested in knowing that because of your help in bringing a problem to our attention, we will not employ again the temporary worker with whom you had a negative interaction.

Please give us another chance to wow you with our service. We have another seminar coming up in Made Up City in April, and we would welcome your attendance. And please come up front to speak with me in April, so you can tell me whether we exceeded your expectations this second time.

With best regards,
Jason Snyder, PhD
Partner, Zimpal Group, LLC

Bearing Good News

One of the most pleasurable responsibilities of a business communicator is that of conveying good news. Taking the opportunity to congratulate, reward, or acknowledge individuals' accomplishments is a fantastic way to build positive relationships inside and outside the workplace. Both of us have received tenure at our respective academic institutions. For those who don't know, tenure is a treasured, honored accomplishment for university faculty members. It doesn't come without a great deal of hard work, talent, and sacrifice, plus a little touch of good luck. When we were awarded tenure, we each received the same form letter from our respective universities. It was short, institutional, impersonal, and legalistic. What a disappointment! When you have the opportunity to bear good news, do so with enthusiasm, charm, and lavish praise. The following is an example of what we recommend.

Sample Letter Delivering Good News

Zimpal Group, LLC
1028 Boulevard
Box 314
West Hartford, CT 06119
860.578.8643

January 31, 2014
Ms. Sheree Sherazod
1234 Maple ST
Made Up City, CT 12345-678

Dear Ms. Sherazod—

Thank you for attending our seminar last month in Made Up City, CT. We are delighted to share the news with you that you are the lucky winner of two round-trip airline tickets to any place in the Continental United States that Delta Airlines flies. You'll remember that Delta was a cosponsor of our event in Made Up City.

Your letter outlining how our seminar helped you develop your personal brand was selected from among 100 others submitted to the contest. The judging panel was composed of two marketing executives with Delta, two business professors at the University of Whooterville, and two small business owners in West Hartford. The judging panel said that of all the contestants, your letter was "the clearest, most compelling demonstration of applying Zimpal's seminar advice to craft a personal brand and target a particular niche for selling your personal services as a graphic designer."

You'll find additional information from Delta on how to redeem your travel vouchers enclosed with this letter. We wish you safe travels and best wishes for continued career success.

Sincerely,
Jason Snyder and Robert Forbus
Partners, Zimpal Group, LLC

Writing a Memorable Thank-You Note

Google "Jackie Kennedy" and "thank you notes," and you'll get about 95,000 hits. The point, here, is that the internationally famous, elegant, trendsetting, polished former first lady of the United States, who was also a book editor in her later years, was famous for her handwritten, highly personalized thank-you notes. Both of us keep stacks of plain, beige-colored fold-over cards and matching envelopes in our respective desks at our individual universities and homes. We both believe, as did Mrs. Kennedy, that handwritten thank-you notes are foundational to good manners. We also have learned through our individual experiences that these notes are appreciated by the receivers and that they differentiate our personal and professional brands from those of others.

Oh, sure, you could just dash off an email. But, really, is that approach enough? We argue that it is not enough. In this age of electronic, instantaneous communication and over-sharing on Facebook, the handwritten thank-you note has taken a seat at the back of the city bus. We're campaigning to bring back the handwritten thank-you note. Here are three simple reasons for our campaign:

1. Most snail mail is computer generated. A handwritten note, on plain, high-quality paper in a matching envelope stands out from the other mail. It gets noticed and gets you noticed.

2. The time it takes to handwrite a thank-you note says that you are an exceptional individual.

3. Job candidates who go to the effort to send a handwritten thank-you note (never on a pre printed thank-you card) demonstrate their attention to detail and their commitment to their professional brand that impresses hiring managers.

Sample Letter of Thanks

Dear Ms. Sherazod,

Your presentation yesterday at Zimpal Group's seminar in downtown Hartford was incredibly well received by those attending. Both the quantitative scores on your portion of the event and the qualitative comments the attendees provided demonstrated the positive impact of your session. It would be impossible for Zimpal to conduct its seminars without individuals such as you providing their time and expertise as presenters and facilitators. As a token of our appreciation for your time and your talent, we have made a contribution to your favorite charity: Fund to Fight World Hunger.

Warmly,

Jason Snyder and Robert Forbus

Writing a Resignation Letter

Back in 1977, the late country music performer Johnny Paycheck had a huge hit in his song "Take This Job and Shove It." The line that followed was "I ain't workin' here no more." While the song's grammar is awful and the sentiment is crass, there aren't too many of us who haven't felt similarly at some point at one or more of our jobs. The song expresses the disappointment and bitterness that can result from working very hard on a job but not being appreciated or appropriately compensated.

At some point in your career, you'll probably have an opportunity to write a resignation letter. This important document is not the place for you to elaborate upon your disappointment and bitterness. This letter should be brief, to the point, and positive. Make sure to check your employing organization's rules about resignations and giving notice. The sample letter we provide is for our firm, which requires a two-week notice. On your way out the metaphorical door of the organization, never forget that you have no idea who is working there who might be able to lock or unlock the door to a position you want in the future. Be gracious in your resignation, and don't make enemies.

Sample Letter of Resignation

Zimpal Group, LLC
1028 Boulevard
Box 314
West Hartford, CT 06119
860.578.8643

January 31, 2014

Dear Drs. Snyder and Forbus,

I write to you with mixed emotions. Two years ago, you provided me an opportunity to launch my career after I completed my MBA. Please know that I am grateful for the many positive learning and working experiences from the past 2 years. Recently, however, an opportunity for a management position came to my attention, one that allows me to build upon my experiences at Zimpal. Therefore, I applied and was the successful candidate. I begin my new role on February 17. My last day with you will be February 14—Valentine's Day, of all days.

Please know that I am committed to helping assure a smooth transition. You will, no doubt, need to meet with me about the status of my ongoing projects. You can depend on me going forward as you have in the past to be an effective member of the Zimpal Group.

Sincerely,
Sheree Sherazod

Writing a Message of Congratulations

Just as much fun as conveying good news is the opportunity to congratulate people on significant accomplishments, career milestones, marriages, the birth of children, and so forth. We both believe these messages go a long way toward maintaining positive relationships in business. Don't limit these messages to your colleagues in your workplace. Look for opportunities to send these messages to people with whom you are building or maintaining a professional relationship within your career network.

Sample Letter of Congratulations

Zimpal Group, LLC
1028 Boulevard
Box 314
West Hartford, CT 06119

January 31, 2014
Ms. Sheree Sherazod
1234 Maple ST
Made Up City, CT 12345-678

Dear Ms. Sherazod—

Congratulations on your recent selection as "Business Woman of the Year." The article in the *Hartford Business Gazette* about your receiving this tremendous honor was a terrific piece of journalism, and it certainly explained clearly why you were chosen. Your generous support of the Fund to Fight World Hunger is just as impressive as your 2-year turnaround of the Acme Automobile Manufacturing Co. Taking such a large firm from red to black ink in just 2 years is spectacular.

Best wishes for continued success at Acme, and thank you for setting such a wonderful example for young business professionals everywhere. Just thinking about the way you are able to do right by your shareholders, while helping people who are less fortunate, all while also being an engaged and involved mother to three growing boys leaves me (and probably most men) exhausted.

Warm regards,
Robert Forbus, PhD
Partner, Zimpal Group, LLC

Writing a Message of Condolence

As we told you earlier, we both keep stacks of plain, beige-colored fold-over cards and matching envelopes in our desks. These cards are perfect for sending messages of condolence to individuals who have experienced the death of a loved one. We don't recommend pre printed condolence cards from, for example Hallmark, for one reason: These are beautiful, but impersonal.

Rather, we encourage you to write from the heart. Make your condolences as personal as you appropriately can to demonstrate your empathy. People are often at their worst when grieving, and communicating with the bereaved can be challenging. Further, we don't always know about the religious or spiritual beliefs of individuals who have experienced the death of someone close to them; consequently, navigating these waters can be a trial. You may prefer to refer to someone's death in a flowery, euphemistic way such as having "passed," or having "expired." We prefer the precision of the words "death" and "died." After all, you can call a dog a "cat," but it makes the dog no more of a feline and no less of a canine.

Below, you'll find a sample message of condolence that is appropriate for business. It is nonreligious and absent of euphemism.

Sample Message of Condolence

Dear Sheree,

We were sorry to learn about the death of your father, James. Though we didn't have the pleasure of knowing him, we believe he must have been a fine man to have brought up such a wonderful person as you are. We know that the process of grieving takes time, and while others' lives move forward the bereaved sometimes can feel as if they are stuck, standing still. Please know that we care, and if you start feeling stuck, and need someone to listen, you can count on us.

Warm regards,
Jason Snyder and Robert Forbus
Zimpal Group, LLC

Writing a Complaint Message

Face it: things in the workplace don't always go according to plan. When that situation arises, you can expect complaints from customers or clients.

Sometimes, you may be in the position of writing a letter of complaint. As with all business communication, these letters should be accurate, brief, and clear (the ABC of business communication). They may be crafted in the form of an email or a snail mail letter. But regardless of the format, there is an additional important point to remember, and that is this: always ask for an action to be taken in your letter of complaint. You are seeking not only to complain about a problem, but also to ask for redress. Below, you'll find a letter of complaint written to us at Zimpal. It would be the letter that prompted Jason's response in the example of communicating bad news.

Sample Letter of Complaint

January 31, 2013
Drs. Jason Snyder and Robert Forbus
Partners
Zimpal Group LLC
1028 Boulevard
Box 314
West Hartford, CT 06119

Dear Drs. Snyder and Forbus,

I attended your seminar on personal branding last month in Made Up City, CT. Your registration procedures were not up to appropriate standards. In fact, I've read your textbook, and frankly I was surprised that your employee, Ralph Goofoff was so rude and seemed to follow none of the advice you give in the pages of your book.

Despite Mr. Goofoff's rudeness to me, which delayed my entry into the room where you were conducting the seminar, I was able to get a seat. It was the last seat in the room. Your seminar was helpful to me. Clearly you know your material. But, the registration experience with Mr. Goofoff ruined the day for me.

I would sincerely appreciate your refunding at least a portion of my seminar fees for the day in light of the poor reception I received at the registration desk.

Sincerely,
Sheree Sherazod

Writing a Reprimanding Message

If you think it is easy to reprimand an employee who has done something wrong, think again. It is an uncomfortable position to be in when we have to tell employees that they aren't performing up to standards, or have been consistently late and must come to work on time, or have violated company policies. Of course, it's uncomfortable for the employee, too, but managers have the additional burden of following company' policies and procedures, most of which are in place to protect the firm from lawsuits.

It's very easy for individuals to sue employers, and while the lawsuit may not make it to court, or if it makes it to court the employee may not win, the resources—time, legal fees, disruption of work, emotional angst—are so intense that we try very hard to avoid lawsuits. Think of Benjamin Franklin's quote: "An ounce of prevention is worth a pound of cure." This 18th century businessman, diplomat, and inventor knew of which he wrote, and it is particularly true when considering employment law.

We do not provide a sample reprimand letter here. However, we urge you to please follow your organization's employment policies and procedures to the letter when dealing with employee problems in the workplace. Document employees' infractions and behaviors in the event you have to face a legal challenge. Follow the good advice of your human resources (HR) director. He or she will be a much better source of information than your gut instinct.

Requesting Information

Today's business professional can write for information in nearly the blink of an eye. Emails and text messages have made short work of asking colleagues, supervisors, direct reports, and others for details on almost any topic. But just because you can do it quickly doesn't mean you are relieved of the responsibility of doing it well. Write in complete sentences, with correct spelling, capitalization, and punctuation when sending either electronic or print requests for information. Follow the sample email below. Always, always write an appropriate subject line when using email. Don't just hit reply to a previous email and start a new message with the former subject line.

Sample Message Requesting Information

To: Jason Snyder
From: Robert Forbus
Date: January 2, 2014
Subject: Textbook stories for chapter 8

Happy New Year, Jason—

I should probably remember, but I have forgotten whether I am responsible for the interviews and stories in chapter 8 of the textbook, or whether you took that job on. Please let me know today, if at all possible. If they are my responsibility, I'd like to finish them by Monday, January 6.

Best—
Robert

Notice that there is a salutation (Happy New Year, Jason —) and a complimentary close (Best —); while this may seem overly formal to you, we remind you that this chapter is devoted to the topic of building and maintaining positive relationships through business communication. The dean in the business school where Robert teaches sets a good example for faculty to follow in her emails, which frequently request information. She always uses a salutation and a complimentary close. And, she always writes with a "you" focus rather than an "I" focus, that is, she writes with the reader in mind.

Writing a Recommendation Message

At a certain point in your career, you will be in a position to write letters of recommendation for coworkers or direct reports who are seeking admission into graduate school or applying for a job. These letters are really important and require careful thought, planning, writing, revising, and proofreading prior to sending.

There are certain legal considerations that you should be aware of, and an explanation of them can frequently be acquired through the HR department at your place of employment. If your organization is small, and doesn't have an HR office, a quick eb search will yield valuable information about legal implications. For the most part, legal implications arise from negative recommendations.

The letter below is one that Dr. Forbus wrote for an MBA student who was seeking a new position. The candidate's name is redacted, but the letter is a good example of a positive recommendation, and one which involved careful thought, planning, writing, revising, and proofreading prior to mailing.

Sample Letter of Recommendation

December 13, 2012
LEX Products Corporation
15 Progress Drive
Shelton, CT 06484

Dear LEX Products Corporation:

_____ is a candidate for the position of Mechanical Project Engineer with your firm. I write in unqualified support of his candidacy.

Mr. ___ was my student in MBA 505 (Marketing Management) at Southern Connecticut State University. He stands out in my memory for multiple reasons: (1) quality of his deliverables; (2) quality of his intellectual contributions to class discussions; and, (3) quality of his analytical skills.

Like many students coming into an MBA program from a non business discipline, Mr. _____, an engineer, entered my classroom overly cautious because of his skepticism about marketing. By his own admission, he didn't have much respect for marketers or for the marketing discipline. Over the course of the semester, little by little, I saw a change in Mr. _____'s thinking. Through reading, emails with me, and stimulating disagreements in class, he began to appreciate that marketing is part science and part art. This fact seemed to appeal to Mr.'s left-brain dominant academic training and professional experience.

Mr._____'s deliverables, including his strategic marketing plan for a new product, his analytical response papers to theoretical and applied marketing topics, and his in-class presentations, demonstrated an open mind, an impressive sense of humor, a mature intellect, and a willingness to challenge his own assumptions. His deliverables also demonstrated a keen intellect and a native curiosity that were both challenging and stimulating to both his professor and his fellow students. Mr._____'s intellectual contributions to classes were unapologetically challenging and unfailingly well informed. Finally, Mr. ____'s analytical skills were masterfully demonstrated and impressively thorough, while appropriately nuanced.

In conclusion, Mr. _____ is young. He has talent, skill, ability, and potential. With the appropriate mentors and opportunities, Mr._____'s aptitude for success is virtually boundless. Feel free to contact me via email forbusr1@southernct.edu or phone 203-XXX-XXXX to discuss Mr. _____'s qualifications in greater detail.

Best regards,
Robert Forbus, PhD
Associate Professor of Marketing

CHAPTER 5

Why Must I Master Report Writing?

Our friend Jeffrey Kotz, whom you met in Chapter 3, holds a Master's degree in marketing communication and has considerable experience in marketing and research analytics. He recently shared a story with us that highlights the need to master report writing. A few years ago, Jeff created a report for a client. The client, a national restaurant chain, sent a senior vice president (SVP) to represent the firm's needs to Jeff's employer, a mid-sized marketing research firm. The SVP asked Jeff and his colleagues to conduct a menu evaluation study. Being a customer-centric organization, the marketing research team conducted a large-scale study of customers, and then developed a report that provided an objective assessment of the restaurant's menu.

As instructed, the team presented a series of recommendations for improving the restaurant chain's menu, based upon the objective assessment. Although the report accomplished the goals provided to the research team, the client ultimately trashed the report. Why? Because the SVP failed to consider the ultimate audience for the report—the franchise owners, who did not want an objective assessment of their restaurants' menu. Given the franchise contract, they could do nothing with that information. They wanted to know how they could capitalize on the current menu to beat their competition. As Jeff put it, "We had much of the information that the franchise owners wanted, but because we were not told about the audience up front, we didn't include relevant information in the report."[1]

The moral of this story should be quite clear—when you don't know your audience, it is difficult to give the audience what it wants, and your chances of success go down. Further, before writing one word of a business report, you must consider who will be the audience for the report.

Mastering report writing starts with knowing your purpose and your audience. To do otherwise imperils your good effort to a bad outcome. Please refer to Chapter 3 for more on understanding your audience.

We've both worked inside and outside of higher education. Regardless of the industries in which we've been employed, we wrote reports—lots of them. And we were not alone. Bodell (2012), writing for *Fast Company*, quoted a Boston Consulting Group study that indicated: "managers spend 40% of their time writing reports and 30% to 60% of it in coordinating meetings."[2] Depending on your job title and function, you may write reports daily, weekly, monthly, or annually.

Regardless of the type of report you are writing, remember the three alphabetical letters we discussed in Chapter 4: A, B, and C. Those letters stand for accurate, brief, and clear. When your report is A, B, and C, your reader may consume the important information easily. Business reports cover an array of topics and have a plethora of objectives. Typical business reports include the following, but please understand the list is far from exhaustive:

- Annual reports
- Annual employment reviews
- Audit reports
- Budget requests
- Feasibility studies
- Government regulatory reports
- Compliance reports
- Sales reports
- Status updates

While Microsoft Word and other products offer templates for report writing, we discourage their use. Likewise, we encourage you to avoid downloading a free template from the Internet. We have nothing against Microsoft, and we are fine with the Internet templates filling your inbox with unsolicited advertising. Even so, we steer you away from templates in general. Why? Because they tend to have a standard look to them, and they are challenging for many users to manipulate because of built-in auto-formatting.

Initial Questionnaire

1. Who will read this report?
2. Why will that person/those people read this report?
3. What is the intent/objective/purpose of writing this report?
4. What are the problems, if any, that I must address in this report?
5. What do I want the reader of the report to know, learn, remember, or do?
6. What are the physical and intellectual resources I need to write the report successfully?

Figure 5.1 Report-writing questionnaire

Rather than using a pre designed template, we suggest you do a bit of research and learn how reports are formatted in your organization. Often, there are standardized formats you are expected or required to use. Sometimes, reports are printed on company letterhead. Other times, you might wish to insert into the header or footer the logo of your organization or the logo of an external organization for which you are creating the report.

Once you've determined the expectations for the appearance of the report, you are ready to move to the next step—your initial questionnaire. Build your initial questionnaire (see Figure 5.1) and answer the questions before you ever write one word of the report's outline.

Never-Fail Outline for Business Reports

Now that you have the answers to the questions from your initial questionnaire, you are ready to build an outline. While every report is different, there are some parts of the report that are relatively standard. Those pieces are laid out for you below:

1. **Executive Summary**—While this section is the first in the report, it will be the last thing you write. If you remember nothing else, remember this: Often, the only parts of a report or proposal that the executive reads are the Executive Summary and the Financials. The executive summary should capture the who, what, when, where, why, how, and how much of your entire report in no more than two pages, preferably in one page.
2. **Background Information**—This section demonstrates your understanding of the situation, problem, or reason for writing the report.

Here, you'll demonstrate that you've done your due diligence, citing your sources—primary, secondary, or both. Remember: Every time you make a statement of fact, back it up with a citation. In business report writing, no one wants or needs your beliefs, dreams, hopes, or opinions. Readers need verifiable facts.

3. **Analyses and Conclusions**—This section demonstrates your capacity to synthesize a large amount of information and provide clear analysis of that information. Not to be too academic, but the information represents data and those data points may be qualitative or quantitative in nature. The best reports often include both types of data. Further, you will present your conclusions that stem from the analyzed data.

4. **Recommendations**—Here you are making recommendations that are based upon the analysis of the data and the conclusions you reached after the analysis. You are arguing a position in this section. You are attempting to persuade—based upon the strength of your arguments—the reader to do, to think, or to know.

5. **Final Summary**—This section of your report ties to your Executive Summary, reiterates your main points, and often includes a call to action. The savvy business writer thinks of the Final Summary as completing the report, just like the bow on a birthday present completes the gift-wrapped package.

Because the vast majority of business reports require you to analyze some sort of data and make recommendations based upon data, we often refer to them as analytical reports. However, in Figures 5.2 and 5.3 are a few reminders about writing effective business reports.

- You do more than merely describe a problem or situation.
- You are not performing a data dump.
- You are not writing about your opinion.
- You are providing readers with an unbiased look at a situation or problem.
- You are drawing informed conclusions.
- You are making logical recommendations based on thorough research, sufficient data, and critical thinking.

Figure 5.2 Reminders for effective business reports

- Readers want to know that you understand your topic and understand their informational needs.
- Readers want to trust your report.
- Conclusions and recommendations are not the same thing.
- Recommendations follow from the data.
- Ideas, recommendations, and action plans are actionable.
- Outcomes need to be measured. You tell the reader how to measure them.
- Recommendations should include SMART goals (specific, measurable, achievable, realistic, time-bound). Think of these as strategic, rather than tactical.
- Objectives are tactical actions that support your goals.
- Goals and objectives always support the organizational mission.
- Recommendations always support the organization's progress toward accomplishing its mission, goals, and objective.
- Claims are supported by evidence. (The sky is blue. We know the sky is blue because. . .)
- Writing is well-organized and visually appealing to make the reader want to read the report.
- Citations for both quoted and paraphrased information prevent unintentional plagiarism.
- Multiple sources boost your credibility. One source is never enough.
- Use both primary and secondary sources of data as appropriate.
- Use both qualitative and quantitative data as appropriate.
- Use only data on which you are willing to risk your professional reputation.
- Bad data lead to bad reports.
- Word misuse is a crime punishable by a fine or imprisonment!

Figure 5.3 Things to remember when writing business reports

Strategic Planning

Strategic plans are a type of business report. Many of you will need to master strategic planning during your careers, so we are devoting a good portion of this chapter to the strategic plan. Here is a quote we like a great deal: "Plans are worthless. *Planning* is everything." Those words came from former U.S. President and World War II General Dwight D. Eisenhower. What did the former President mean? He probably meant that plans don't guarantee success, but the planning process allows us to anticipate possible problems and take appropriate actions so that success is far more likely than would be possible without planning.

Why is this useful in business? It helps us to be more effective and most efficient. Strategic plans are an important part of what businesses do, and should be carried out with meticulous attention to detail. You'll notice many similarities between the strategic plan outline and the outline above for business reports. There is a key difference, however. Strategic planning focuses on mission, goals, and objectives. Let's take a look at the outline that follows.

Executive Summary

Please see the advice from our outline above. Your executive summary should include the following:

- business or organization's name;
- business or organization's location;
- purpose of the strategic plan;
- organization's mission and how this strategic plan supports the mission;
- important points, such as projected sales or organizational changes;
- graphical elements to help your reader "see" what you propose; bar charts, line graphs, and other similar elements can be extremely effective here;
- evaluation times/activities/methods (remember, you must be able to measure/quantify your results, which are sometimes called "outcomes");
- cost of implementing the plan and projected outcomes.

Research

No matter what kind of strategic planning activity you're involved in, research will be at the core of it. Depending on what you're doing, different research methods can be used at various times. Research methods are categorized into two groups.

Primary

This is finding out the information you want first hand: questionnaires, one-to-one interviews, telephone interviews, focus groups, blogs, and so forth. Your plan will outline a proposed original research activity.

Secondary

This involves gathering information from sources other than your own, original research. Examples include books, academic and other journals, newspapers, magazines, libraries, electronic databases, sales figures, the Internet, and so forth.

Situation Analysis

This section of the plan should provide an overview of where your firm or organization is, both externally and internally. Furthermore, it needs to forecast trends in the dynamic environment in which it operates. You will cover many, or perhaps all, of the following elements in your situation analysis.

Company

- Product line/Product category (*NAICS/SIC, which are standardized industry codes, are often helpful to use in these reports. You'll find these industry codes at http://www.naics.com/search.htm*)
- Image in the market
- Technology and experience
- Culture
- Goals

Collaborators

- Distributors
- Suppliers
- Alliances

Customers

- Market size and growth
- Market segments
- Benefits that consumers seek, both tangible and intangible
- Motivation behind purchase; value drivers, benefits versus costs
- Decision maker or decision-making unit
- Retail channel—where does the consumer actually purchase the product?

- Consumer information sources—where does the customer obtain information about the product?
- Buying process; for example, impulse or careful comparison
- Frequency of purchase, seasonal factors
- Quantity purchased at a time
- Trends—how consumer needs and preferences change over time

Competitors

- Actual or potential
- Direct or indirect
- Products
- Positioning
- Market share
- Strengths and weaknesses of competitors

Climate (or Context)

The climate or macroenvironmental factors include the following:

- Political and regulatory environment—governmental policies and regulations that affect the market
- Economic environment—business cycle, inflation rate, interest rates, and other macroeconomic issues
- Social/Cultural environment—society's trends and fashions
- Technological environment—new knowledge that makes possible new ways of satisfying needs; the impact of technology on the demand for existing products

SWOT Analysis

SWOT is an acronym made up of the first letters of the following words: strengths, weaknesses, opportunities, and threats. It grows out of your situation analysis. You must clearly define the current situation that your organization faces and closely relate your planned strategy. A good place for you to start is to find a "real" SWOT analysis that has been completed for an organization and follow that SWOT as a template.

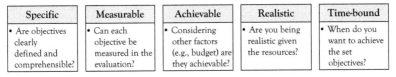

Specific	Measurable	Achievable	Realistic	Time-bound
• Are objectives clearly defined and comprehensible?	• Can each objective be measured in the evaluation?	• Considering other factors (e.g., budget) are they achievable?	• Are you being realistic given the resources?	• When do you want to achieve the set objectives?

Figure 5.4 SMART objectives

Goals and Objectives

Once you're aware of the problem(s) your organization is facing, you can then define the goals and objectives of the strategic plan. The goals will be broad and somewhat aspirational. The objectives are what you intend to achieve through your strategic plan. Each objective must be SMART, which is an acronym we define in Figure 5.4.

Identifying Publics

Whom do you want to talk to? The research carried out in the initial stages of the planning process should have identified each public relevant to the plan. This is crucial to ensure your key messages are communicated efficiently as possible. The research also should have identified each public's current attitude to the situation, allowing you to tailor your key messages appropriately.

Identifying Stakeholders

Once the publics of this plan have been categorized, it is then important to identify who the stakeholders are. A stakeholder analysis is not as specific as identifying publics as it looks at everyone that is involved in the plan as opposed to only those who need to be communicated to. Publics can be categorized as a particular type of stakeholder. A stakeholder analysis may involve the following:

- Employees
- Identified publics
- Suppliers
- Senior executives
- Investors
- Others

Strategy

Strategy is often confused with the tactics. However, the strategy is the foundation on which a tactical (activities) program is built. Think of it this way: the strategy is winning a war, while the tactics are the battles you may fight to win that war. The strategy is usually the big picture, overlying mechanism of a plan from which the tactics are deployed to meet the objectives. Take a moment to refer to Michael Porter's generic competitive strategies in Figure 5.5.

Tactics

Business professionals have many tactics (or tools) at their disposal. The challenge is choosing the right tactics to meet the objectives. Again, depending on what type of planning you're involved in, you might use media relations, lobbying, events, interviews, blogger relations, presentations, consultations, newsletters, competitions, podcasts, stunts, websites, conferences, photography, video news releases, and so forth.

Remember, don't use newfangled tactics because they are perceived to be cool, cutting-edge, or the "in" thing. Use only the tools that will best help you meet your objectives. With that stated, remember that creativity is always important.

Time Line

Once you know the strategy you'll use and the tactics you'll deploy, you must determine a schedule for conducting the plan you've created. A time line allows you to coordinate your tactics appropriately and helps you be aware of deadlines. Not only that, if there are certain future events that relate to your plan, you can tailor a tactic in your time line to coincide. Evaluation should be part of your time line, and not only once at the end of the project.

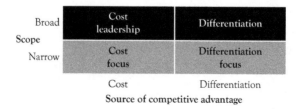

Figure 5.5 Michael Porter's competitive strategies

Budget

Allocating the budget is an essential part of strategic planning. All costs should be taken into consideration. Salaries and benefits, however, are sometimes not part of the budget, especially if you are doing strategic planning in communications or marketing or some other functional area of business. These items aren't part of a marketing plan. The primary reason for a budget is to let you know what you can or can't do, based on the funds available. It also allows you to allocate money to the specific areas of the plan. Make your budget realistic, and provide a break-even analysis in your budget.

Evaluation

Though placed last, it would be useful to have at least three evaluation points in your strategic plan. Therefore, you must decide how and when to execute three evaluations of your progress toward your goals. Evaluation is an ongoing process, particularly in a long-term strategic plan, so it is critical to constantly review all specific elements (tactics) to see how you are progressing toward accomplishing your goal (strategy). Evaluation is vital to discover which parts of the strategic plan are successful and which are not. Not only that, it helps determine what the current situation is after the tactics/activities have ended, in comparison to what the situation was before you implemented your plan.

Conclusion

Now that you've worked through this chapter on report writing and gotten a crash course on strategic planning as a type of business report, we hope you understand clearly the answer to this chapter's question: *Why Must I Master Report Writing?* The answer is simple: To succeed in your career, you will have to master this important skill. Organizations make decisions based on reports. Reports are not easy to write and involve both risk and reward. Many workers try to avoid writing reports for these very reasons. But, professionals who hone their report-writing skills and volunteer for such opportunities make themselves invaluable to their organizations.

CHAPTER 6

Why Must I Remember the Four "F" Words?

Military personnel and their families make unbelievable sacrifices for their countries, and no sacrifice is greater than the loss of a soldier's life. Imagine being the mother of a member of the military. Imagine the conflicting emotions of pride and anguish as your son or daughter is sent to a foreign country to fight in a war. Imagine the heart-wrenching pain of learning that your son or daughter was killed while defending your country. Imagine receiving a handwritten letter from your nation's commander-in-chief to discover that your child's name is spelled incorrectly. Imagine how insulted you would feel by the lack of sensitivity.

Unfortunately, Jacqui Janes, a mother in Great Britain, does not have to imagine this situation. It is precisely what happened to her in 2009, when the then Prime Minister Gordon Brown mailed a letter of condolence to Mrs. Janes following the death of her son in Afghanistan. In her outrage, Mrs. Janes sent the letter to the media and also recorded a phone conversation she had with the Prime Minister in which she berated him for his lack of sensitivity.[1]

Ultimately, the Prime Minister apologized to Mrs. Janes for his sloppy handwriting. Those people most sympathetic to Mr. Brown likely believe that some of the errors in the letter could have resulted from a vision problem. They are also likely to believe that the Prime Minister did not intend to act disrespectfully in this situation. In fact, how many world leaders take the time to write handwritten notes to the families of fallen soldiers? It is entirely possible that Mr. Brown was sincere in his condolence. Unfortunately, his intended message was negated because he did not proofread and revise his letter.[2]

The next time you ask yourself why it is so important to proofread and revise your writing, think about Mr. Brown, think about Jacqui Janes, and

Message 1
Dear Colleagues,

It is with sadness that I ask you to join me to convey our condolences to FEMALE EMPLOYEE. Her mother passed away on XXXX. We share her pain and have her and her family in our prayers. Additional information will be forwarded to you as we receive it.

Best,
Organizational Leader

Message 2
Dear Colleagues,

It is with sadness again that I ask you to join me to convey our condolences to MALE EMPLOYEE. His mother-in-law passed away last week. We share her pain and have her and her family in our prayers. Additional information will be forwarded to you as we receive it.

Best,
Organizational Leader

Figure 6.1 Insincere condolence messages?

most importantly, think about her son Jamie Janes. When others shrug off the ideas of proofreading and revising, share this story with them.

So you don't see yourself in the position of Prime Minister? Proofreading and revising are still important. For example, look at the two email messages in Figure 6.1. These emails were sent to the members of a leader's organization. Unfortunately, two members of the organization experienced personal tragedy. In a sincere effort to inform the other members and pass along condolences to the affected members, the leader sent out these two emails within 16 minutes of one another. If you are a worker reading the first message, it would likely come off as direct and sincere. However, in light of the cut-and-paste job with the glaring typo (sentence three) in the second email, both messages come off as insincere. It is not unusual for leaders to use message templates, but the third sentence of the second message undermines the leader's intent for both messages.

Proofreading, Revising, and Your Professional Reputation

If you're like us, you don't want a lack of proofreading to undermine your message or your credibility. Although we aren't perfect, we must all understand that when we fail to proofread and revise our written work, there comes a point when the work is more about the errors than the message.

Anne Grinols, a well-respected professor of business communication, delivered a presentation at the Annual Convention of the Association for Business Communication in 2010 about the importance of proofreading. She shared with the audience a demonstration that drives home the point about errors undermining our messages.

Grinols told us to think about our writing the same way we do about drinking water. Imagine a hot summer day. Your friend has been toiling away in the yard pulling weeds and tending to the garden. She asks you for a drink of water. So you go to the tap and pour a glass of water for your friend. In this scenario, the friend should be delighted to accept the clear, crisp water. We hope in business writing that our readers feel the same way about our prose—they should be happy and the message should be clear and crisp.

But what if, just before handing the water to your friend, you stir a teaspoon of dirt into the water? How do you think your friend would respond? What if you stirred in two teaspoons of dirt? Would your friend still be happy to accept the water? Would your friend drink the water? At what point does the glass of water become more about the dirt and less about the water?

If we think about errors in our writing as pieces of dirt, we have to ask at what point is a message more about the errors and less about the content. And over time, what does the accumulation of errors say about us as professionals? We all make mistakes but polished professionals work diligently to make that number as small as possible. People prefer to drink water that has been thoroughly filtered. They like their messages to be similarly filtered.[3]

In this chapter, we will share with you a four-step process that we use to proofread and revise our written work. The process can be used to evaluate just about any piece of written work, including emails, memos, letters, and reports. Although many people may use one "F" word when they think about proofreading and revising, we prefer to use four "F" words: Format, Filling, Feeling, and Filth.

The Four "F" Words of Proofreading and Revising

F1: *Format*

In the first step of the four-step process, you should take a global view of the document. Don't jump right into proofreading for grammar errors. First, you should ask yourself if the document "looks right," because in writing, just as in beauty pageants, looks matter. Determine if the document has been formatted appropriately. Here are some questions you can ask yourself as you look over the document.

Does the Document Meet Your Organization's Standards?

The first thing you should determine is if you have formatted the document to meet your organization's standards. Some organizations provide employees with templates and writing guides to ensure that messages have a consistent look.

Do the Key Ideas Jump Off the Page?

As we mentioned in Chapter 1, today's working professionals are busy and suffering from information overload. They do not read everything that comes across their desks. They use selective perception to determine what is important and they *skim*. So ask yourself. If someone were quickly glancing at your document, would it pass the skim test? Can you quickly identify the key ideas?

What can you do to make sure that your ideas do jump off the page? Thankfully, we have a number of mechanical devices at our disposal to help us format our documents in a way that makes the ideas jump off the page. For example, we can write important ideas in **bold**, *italic*, <u>underlined</u>, or <u>***a combination***</u> of font styles. In addition, you can use one or more of the following (but be careful not to overuse):

- Bulleted and enumerated lists
- Color
- Tables and figures
- ALL CAPS
- Headings and subheadings.

Is the Document Readable?

Readability refers to how easily a message can be read and understood. One of the easiest ways to enhance a document's readability is to avoid what we call the WALL OF WORDS effect. You are familiar with wall of words documents; they are the documents that have long sentences, long paragraphs, and use full justification. Look over your document and make sure that you've made wise use of white space.

To illustrate the points about the first "F" word, let's take a look at a few examples. Figure 6.2 that follows is an executive summary that Jason wrote on behalf of his department. The document summarizes a report for the university's Provost about a project concerning student class attendance. Executive summaries are immensely important because the executives who read them are busy. They may not have the time to read the entire report. So they rely on the executive summary to highlight a report's essential elements. The main points of the report should be easy to find and readily accessible to the reader.

The executive summary in Figure 6.2 could use a little help. It suffers from the wall of words effect. The main points are in the summary, but they certainly don't leap off the page. By comparison, look at Figure 6.3. The content is identical to Figure 6.2, but we made a few minor changes to the executive summary's formatting. Do you see how much more user-friendly the revised document is for the reader?

EXECUTIVE SUMMARY

This report provides you with an update on the Management Information System's GRAD Program (Graduate Rapidly by Attending Daily). In this report you will read about the program's progress, findings from the fall 2011 experiment to decrease class absenteeism, and recommendations for the program moving forward.

This report will summarize the steps taken by the Management Information Systems Department to create a culture that values class attendance. In addition, we will describe an experiment about compulsory attendance policies conducted in MIS 201 and MC 207 classes. We will present an analysis of this data and describe actions that faculty will take during spring 2012 semester.

Use of compulsory attendance policies resulted in a dramatic reduction in class absenteeism. Students who were in a class with a compulsory attendance policy missed less than half the number of classes compared to students who were in a class with no compulsory attendance policy. Students who missed fewer classes earned much higher grades than students who missed more classes. Students in both MIS 201 and MC 207 – two very different courses – responded to compulsory attendance policies by missing fewer classes than students in classes without a compulsory attendance policy.

Based on the key findings, the faculty in the Management Information Systems Department will undertake the following four-part plan for spring 2012: 1) Adopt the compulsory attendance policy in MC 207, 2) Collect additional data in MIS 201 to determine the impact of the same instructor using different policies, 3) Discuss new ways to advertise and promote the program, and 4) Conduct analysis of survey data.

Figure 6.2 Poorly formatted executive summary

EXECUTIVE SUMMARY

Purpose
This report provides you with an update on the Management Information System's GRAD Program (Graduate Rapidly by Attending Daily). In this report you will read about the program's progress, findings from the fall 2011 experiment to decrease class absenteeism, and recommendations for the program moving forward.

Background, Research, and Analysis
This report will summarize the steps taken by the Management Information Systems Department to create a culture that values class attendance. In addition, we will describe an experiment about compulsory attendance policies conducted in MIS 201 and MC 207 classes. We will present an analysis of this data and describe actions that faculty will take during spring 2012 semester.

Key Findings
- Use of compulsory attendance policies resulted in a dramatic reduction in class absenteeism. Students who were in a class with a compulsory attendance policy missed less than half the number of classes compared to students who were in a class with no compulsory attendance policy.

- Students who missed fewer classes earned much higher grades than students who missed more classes.

- Students in both MIS 201 and MC 207 – two very different courses – responded to compulsory attendance policies by missing fewer classes than students in classes without a compulsory attendance policy.

Spring 2012 Plan
Based on the key findings, the faculty in the Management Information Systems Department will undertake the following four-part plan for spring 2012:

1. Adopt the compulsory attendance policy in MC 207

2. Collect additional data in MIS 201 to determine the impact of the same instructor using different policies

3. Discuss new ways to advertise and promote the program

4. Conduct analysis of survey data.

Figure 6.3 Revised executive summary

Now let's consider a second example. In Figure 6.4, you will see a portion of a memorandum that was written by one of our students. The assignment called for students to interview a professional who was working in the student's desired career field. The students were asked to find out about the role of communication in the interview subject's job. Lessons about communication were to be extracted from the interview data and reported in a brief memorandum. The memorandum in Figure 6.4 can be improved significantly with only a handful of formatting changes. Here are some of the formatting problems:

1. The routing information is not formatted appropriately. The date is floating on the right margin all by itself.
2. The subject line is not indicative of the memo's content. The reader should be able to look at the subject line and have a good idea of the message's purpose and content.

3. The memo suffers from the wall of words effect. Using an unjustified right margin and adding spaces between the paragraphs would make the document more readable.

4. The main points do not jump from the page. Headings would go a long way toward emphasizing the main points.

In Figure 6.5, you will see a portion of a memorandum written by a different student in the same class. You don't need to be a seasoned communications professional to see the stark difference between this memorandum and the one in Figure 6.4. The memorandum in Figure 6.5 is more appealing to the eye and more user-friendly. The writer used white space effectively, emphasized key points with headings, and wrote a clear

MEMORANDUM

To: Dr. Jason L. Snyder   Date: January 13, █████

From: █████████████

Subject: Interview a Communications Expert

Per your request, I have interviewed a communications expert for the purposes of understanding the importance of communications in the working environment. The first person who came to my mind when you presented this project to the class was ██████ █████ Director of Communications of the Department of Revenue Services (DRS). She was gracious enough to provide to me her time and knowledge.

█████ has been working at DRS for nine years. Prior to her arrival, there was no designated communications expert. When █████ came to DRS, it was a time where her skills and resources were very much needed at DRS. The agency was going through many changes with the enactment of the income tax and our agency was inevitably growing. The need for professional external communications was rapidly growing with numerous publications and instructions being disseminated to the public as well as news alerts for swift changes in tax law and the demand by media for headline news stories. Internal communication became a necessity as well as we needed to utilize our current staff to produce massive amounts of literature and create processes to accomplish forms and tax return approval. Sarah has been an integral participant in the processes that are still used today to accomplish changes in DRS's structure and handling of tax law amendments

█████ came to DRS with experience in the communications field as she worked in public relations and research for the Connecticut General Assembly and was also a newspaper reporter. Nonetheless, she learned many lessons in her current responsibilities that I received as valuable lessons. She stressed the importance of keeping an open mind and realizing that you never stop learning in your job. The best advice she provided was to stay abreast of changes and be informed of your material, in other words, understand the technical aspects for which you are writing about. She also found it challenging to write on someone else's behalf, finding their voice and learning their style, as occasionally she ghost writes letters on the Commissioner's behalf. She can overcome that challenge by keeping the language professional and to the point.

Figure 6.4 Poorly formatted memorandum

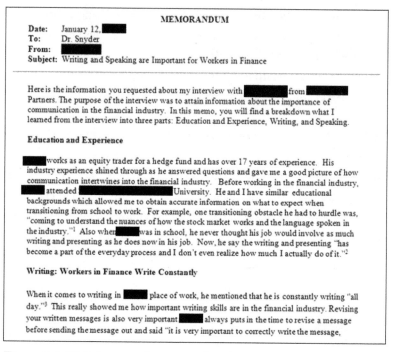

Figure 6.5 *Well-formatted memorandum*

and descriptive subject line. Any reader would need only to skim the document to have a clear idea of the memorandum's purpose.

F2: Filling

Now that you've made certain that your document is beautifully formatted, turn your attention to the second step of the four-step process. In this step, you should review the content of your document. Again, you aren't proofreading for grammar errors. Instead, you are evaluating your message to determine if it has the appropriate content, or filling. In doing so, you will want to answer a few questions.

Is the Purpose Clear?

Everything you write should be driven by a purpose. Do you know what you want your reader to know, do, or believe after she has finished reading your document? Too often, unpolished professionals make mistakes that could be easily avoided if they first thought about their purpose. A document's purpose is a lot like a company's mission statement. It provides a reason for the document's existence and drives strategic decisions in the writing process. If a writer can't state her document's purpose, how can she expect her reader to understand it?

Is all Necessary Information Included and Organized?

Answering this question effectively requires that you first have a few key pieces of information yourself. First, you need to have sufficient content knowledge about the message's topic. Do your research. Make sure you have collected information from credible primary and secondary sources and that you have both quantitative and qualitative information. When you make claims, you will need the evidence to support them. Look at your document. Do you provide sufficient and credible support for your claims? Moreover, how can you expect to meet your audience's information needs if you don't know the topic thoroughly? You wouldn't be too successful selling Kentucky Fried Chicken a deep fryer if you didn't know anything about preparing fried chicken.

In addition to sufficient content knowledge, you also need to understand your audience thoroughly. You need to determine what information they have and what information they need. Good writers anticipate audience questions and try to answer them. Because most of our business communications are strategic and aimed at getting a response from our audience, we need to understand what our audience cares about.

It is important that we answer not only their content questions but also speak to their interests. We must answer the WIIFY question that all audiences care about—What's In It For You? If you want your audience to adopt a new perspective, take your advice, or change behavior, you better be able to tell them what they can expect to get from the transaction. As college professors, we receive requests from students who want us to open up extra seats in our classes for them. Too often, the students' arguments focus solely on their rationale for needing the class, such as graduating on time or fulfilling a prerequisite for other classes. We're not entirely heartless, but from our perspective, we have a limited number of openings in our classes and adding students results in more work for us. Students who don't answer our WIIFY question are less likely to get one of those precious few seats.

To be convincing, we also need to understand what forces will move our audiences to saying yes to our requests and what forces are holding them back from saying yes. Anne Grinols once referred to these forces as driving and restraining forces. Your document is not complete unless you have addressed your audience's driving and restraining forces.[4]

It is also important that you understand how your audience will react to the message. Their response (positive, neutral, negative), as we learned in Chapter 3, will go a long way toward determining how you organize the content of your messages using a direct or indirect approach.

To complicate matters further, in many cases our messages have more than one audience. We need to meet the information needs of multiple audiences simultaneously. Robert Hokunson III works in information technology for a large insurance and financial services organization. One of his current responsibilities is to write application-performance reports, which are designed to report on problems that occur with the company's technical applications. He writes these reports for audiences with differing information needs, high-level executives and application developers. He explains that when a technical application fails, "the executives want answers to questions like: How bad is it, how big of a problem is it, and how are we fixing it? The developers want answers to questions like: How often does it happen, what is causing it, where did it start, and what are the technical details? You have to find the fine line between both audiences. You might need to produce an extra slide in the deck with the technical details that can be skimmed by the executives while answering the developers' questions."[5]

F3: Feeling

Once you are satisfied with your message's format and filling, you can move to the third step of the four-step process. In this step, you are determining whether your message strikes the appropriate tone and treats your audience respectfully. As we learned in Chapter 1, feelings are relevant in business even though we tend to be misguided by the notion that business is rational. Think back to our advice in Chapter 4 where we discussed the importance of building and maintaining *positive* relationships through business communications. When evaluating your document for tone and respect, consider the following things.

Do You Make Polite Requests?

In business communication, we may find ourselves in a one-up position where we must make directives and ask that people complete tasks. When making those requests, look at the document and ask yourself if you've made the request politely. Please and thank you go a long way, even when you're in the position of authority.

Do You Avoid Abstract Words and Phrases?

You might be asking yourself why this question falls under tone and respect. When you use abstract words and phrases, including unnecessarily formal language; jargon; and slang, you may be striking an inappropriate tone. Obviously, there are times when you must use jargon or technical language, but when it isn't necessary, don't use it. Even when it is necessary, make sure you know your audience. Will all your readers understand your message? If you can't say yes, then you're best advised to provide, either in the text or in an appendix, definitions that your readers will understand. It is inconsiderate to use language that your audience will not understand. When writers use words that are needlessly formal or jargon-y, it is easy for their readers to feel turned off. How many adults do you know who enjoy being talked down to?

Are Your Emotions in Check?

When we don't keep our emotions in check, we often make the mistake of giving ourselves a short-term emotional boost at the expense of our message's true purpose. In Figure 6.6, you will find a portion of a student email message that was addressed to a professor. As you can see, the student who wrote the email was likely looking for a change to his or her grade. Unfortunately, in alleviating his or her emotional distress, the writer lost sight of the *real purpose* and also lost control of the message's tone.

i refuse to accept the grade that you gave my group for the final project. i understood completely when i turned it in that it was not going to be an A assignment. how could it be? it was a project designed for 5 people to contribute to and i had one. i was the group leader and maybe it all falls down on poor management skills.. maybe. however i had 3 people in my group who (excuse my language i have taken this very personally) just didnt give a shit about the project. we would discuss days to meet and then they would not show up or they would come empty handed. i am not saying that they did not put forth any effort , i am very confident in their ability to type espn and nascar into a google search bar, but ultimately it comes back to not having read the book all semester. i have no idea but i would almost bet 100 dollars that gia and andrew have very poor quiz scores because they just did not get it. they would show up to meetings with bullet points and could not put anything together. i tried delegating aspects but they would never complete the tasks. i delegated to mark in the beginning the history and he was the only one who came through. He was the only one to do his section. i had the SWOT analysis. which you gave us a zero on. i will take your comments and make the paper better and resubmit to you ... but i did have social and technological factors in there and still got zero points ... i also was looking at it differently seen as all the other groups had actual products .. and we had an entertainment service i thought i was properly adjusting information. regardless i received no other written material from anyone...

Figure 6.6 Emotion-laden email

Do You Make the Effort to Soften the Blow of Bad News?

Delivering bad news is a fact of life in business. We must say no to requests, fire employees, deny promotions, cut relations with vendors, deny customer claims, and write many other uncomfortable messages. In Chapter 4, we provided you with advice on how to write bad news messages. It is our firm belief that one can deliver bad news without being bad. Relationships matter.

F4: Filth

Once you are satisfied that your message strikes the appropriate tone, it is finally time to take a detailed look at spelling, grammar, and mechanics. In this step, we are reviewing our document for fine particulate—in keeping with our dirty water metaphor. We discussed common writing errors at great length in Chapter 3. Here we will provide you with tips for identifying errors like a professional.

Use Word Processing Power

You have access to word processing programs. Use them. Use them carefully. In these programs, you can often modify the settings to identify spelling and grammar errors. As a rule of thumb, when the program identifies an error, you should at least check to see if you've actually made an error. Don't ignore the program. At the same time, don't simply accept whatever changes the program recommends. After all, these programs are designed by programmers, not professional copy editors. As a result, these programs occasionally identify nonexistent problems (i.e., cry wolf), fail to identify real problems (i.e., miss the boat), and offer incorrect solutions to real problems.

For example, our students commonly misspell the word "definite." We don't know how they misspell the word, but we do know that word processing programs will try to fix the error. When these programs try to fix a spelling error, they use the letters provided by the writer to determine what the writer intended to spell. When our students misspell "definite," word processing programs often suggest "defiant." So instead of our students writing that they will "definitely complete" their assignments, they expose their revolutionary roots and tell us they will "defiantly complete" their assignments. Word processing programs are amazing little tools, but like all tools, we must engage our brain while using them, or suffer the consequences.

Get Help

The best writers in the world have editors. If they have other people proofread their work, then you should too. Of course, in business you will find that occasionally your documents contain confidential information and cannot be shared with a trusted editor. When that's the case, apply the following tips:

- *Change the medium.* It is often hard to identify our own errors. We're sure that a few mistakes will probably slip through to the version of this book that you're reading right now. Sorry. One reason why it can be difficult to identify our own errors is that we often try to proofread our documents on the same medium where we originally drafted it. We proofread emails in our email programs, we proofread letters in word processing programs, and we proofread slide presentations in the slide presentation software in which we designed them. Good copy editors shake things up by changing the medium when they proofread. Remember Judith Wenger Weir, the PR professional we discussed in Chapter 4? She also told us about a lesson she learned about proofreading from her boss, a former journalist. She said that she uses Microsoft Word to write documents. So she will print out a copy and proofread the hard copy. She also proofreads PowerPoint materials in Microsoft Word.[6] Take it from people who write for a living, if you want to catch your mistakes, change the medium.

- *Trick yourself.* Another reason why we often miss our own errors is that we don't expect to see them. When you draft a document, you think about what you want to write before you actually write it down. How often does the version in your mind have errors? Based on the ideas of selective perception, if you don't expect to see errors, you won't. One thing you can do to trick yourself and work against selective perception is to proofread your documents from the last line to the first. Start at the end and work to the beginning.
- *Read aloud.* Read your documents aloud. If something doesn't sound right, it probably isn't.

Conclusion

Please remember that nobody is perfect. You want, however, to be the best filter that you can be. By following this four "F" words approach, you will catch many of the little mistakes that will affect your messages and your reputation. If you use these simple tips, you won't become known as the person who asks people to drink dirty water.

CHAPTER 7

Why Must I Give a Memorable Presentation?

In most of our chapters, we rely on the anecdotes of others to introduce a topic. For this chapter, we've decided to share a story from our vault of examples. One of us, who shall remain nameless, but you'll figure out which one of us while you are reading this chapter, once witnessed the worst public presentation ever made. No kidding. The. Worst. Ever.

A young PR executive from Toyota, which had a plant in Alabama (*hint about which author was the witness of this terrible presentation*), was representing her company at a trade show. The venue for the show was the campus of a historically Black university in Montgomery. The executive made several fatal errors that caused her failure. No one else could take responsibility for her mistakes. As a footnote, we'll tell you that we don't know whether she kept her job after her public disgrace; but, we wouldn't be surprised to learn that she left the country in embarrassment and became a subsistence fisherperson in a remote location where she could live incognito.

The first mistake she made was she didn't do her homework. Having done no reconnaissance regarding the facility where she would be presenting, she created a slide show with a Mac Computer, and didn't bother to find out whether the facility where she was to present would have Mac capabilities. She arrived with her presentation burned onto a CD-ROM, which was cutting-edge technology in 1999. *That reference to the year 1999 was another hint about the author who witnessed the crash-and-burn presentation.* Unfortunately for her, the facility where she was presenting had the latest Dell Computers, and there wasn't a Mac in sight.

The second mistake she made was she didn't know her audience. Before creating an outline, writing a word, or creating a slide template, presenters must conduct research to find out the following:

- **Who** is the audience for the presentation?
- **What** position do the audience members hold on the subject of the presentation?
- **What** do the audience members want to know about the presenter's topic?
- **What** will be the demographic composition of the audience?
- **Where** will the presentation be held and what are the location's capabilities?
- **Why** is the presentation needed?
- **How** do the audience members want to be engaged (for example, formally or facilitation format)?

These seven bullet points are the absolute minimum amount of audience research that a presenter must do before ever starting to plan for the presentation.

The third mistake our friend from Toyota made was that she hadn't learned her material. She easily could have recovered from the disastrous technology problem if she had bothered to learn her material. But, alas for her and her audience, she had intended to present from the slides, probably doing little more than reading them to her audience. Clearly nervous, with darting eyes, enlarged pupils, and trembling hands, she approached the microphone behind which she was supposed to enlighten her audience of approximately 200 automotive industry executives about the intricacies of starting an automotive manufacturing plant in Alabama and dealing with the state's government entities. The excruciating pain she felt was witnessed by every audience member, and every audience member felt pain for the presenter. Though she shed no tears, her quivering voice, stammering delivery, and shaking limbs told a story of shame beyond belief.

Young professionals aren't the only ones who make terrible presentations. Judith Wagner Weir, the PR professional from Chapter 4, shares a story about a high-profile public figure who missed the mark during a presentation. "Governor Malloy attended one of our events. It was clear that he hadn't done his research because his message was inappropriate for his audience." Ouch! Governors, presidents, and other important leaders have speechwriters who are paid to make the presenter look good. It is unimaginable that a professional speechwriter would send his or her employer out to make a presentation with a poorly prepared speech.

Judith also witnessed recently another surprisingly bad presentation. "I attended a Public Relations Society of America chapter event that was packed with business professionals. There was a presenter who was supposed to be an expert on using social media. I was eager to learn from her expertise so I could use social media to promote my work. She got stuck in her presentation. Drew a blank. Had no written notes to which she could refer. She was bad." Judith says the woman tried to play off her bad presentation by making a remark that she intended as funny, but it fell flat and confirmed her lack of preparation.

Falling on Your Face

While it is possible that there are more than four reasons you can fall on your face while making a presentation or delivering a speech, we believe we have identified the four major reasons, which are illustrated in Figure 7.1.

These four behaviors are, to some degree interrelated, yet any one of the four can cause a complete disaster. Put all four together, and, well, you might end up in some government program to protect your identity.

Figure 7.1 Four causes of presentation failure

Fear

Fear is a funny thing. A little bit can keep you alert and reactive when faced with danger. A lot can paralyze you and prevent you from responding when faced with danger. Overcoming anxiety and fear of presentations is as simple as rehearse, rehearse, rehearse until you know the material like you know the actors' names in a favorite movie. Remember that fear can create a self-fulfilling prophecy. Are you one of those people who say, "I'm just no good at public speaking?" Although some of us may be better than others, public speaking skills can be honed through practice. If you allow your fear to keep you from delivering presentations, you won't develop the skills, and you will never be good at public speaking. In a world of happy psychology, there is still something to be said about preparing for the worst. Let your fear guide you to being as prepared as possible.[1]

Poor Preparation

This cause and the one that follows are tied inextricably together. The failure to conduct your audience research, to learn your material, and to plan how best to deliver a memorable and compelling presentation are all part of poor preparation. Rehearsal is critical.

Sloth

The animal sloth is kind of cute and the beautiful actress Kristen Bell is obsessed with them. You don't believe us? Google it. Seriously. Sloth in a human, though, means that person is lazy. Don't be a sloth. Kristen would disapprove. Good presentations are the result of hard work.

Lack of Imagination

This book contains many stories because anecdotes help us to learn, help us to personalize material, and help others to remember what we want them to know. You do not have to be an artistic genius to be imaginative. Think through your memories, talk to friends and family members, look at popular culture, do ANYTHING to demonstrate imagination in order to capture and hold your audience's attention. If audience members don't listen or care, they surely won't remember.

We like to teach people about these four causes of presentation failure because they have one thing in common—you have the power to fix them. Too frequently, we blame poor performance on matters beyond our own control. When we blame poor performance on circumstances, then we excuse ourselves of personal responsibility for the failure. Don't fall into that trap. We will all have presentation failures in our careers. The best speakers learn from those experiences and take action to fix the problem in the future.

Getting Started the Right Way

Before you begin preparing your presentation ask yourself this simple question, what is my presentation about? If you answer that question with one or two words, then you skipped Chapter 3, where we talked about purpose statements. We won't force you to go back and read it now, but we do want you to understand one important point. World-class consultant and author Nancy Duarte reminds her followers that presentations are your opportunity to change your part of the world, even in business. Before you start putting together your presentation, you need to identify your "big idea": What idea are you selling to your audience and what are the stakes involved? You need to get out of the routine of saying, "my presentation is about increasing sales." Instead, get into the habit of expressing your big idea with the stakes involved. Try the following: "We need to adopt new sales strategies or we will be driven out of business."[2] Instead of thinking about topics you will discuss, think about how your big ideas will change your world.

Figure 7.2 summarizes a number of techniques you might use to energize the introduction to a presentation.

Supercharging Your Introduction

How many times have you witnessed someone who gets up before a group, gives his or her name, states the topic, and launches immediately

1. Ask a question	6. Make a startling statement
2. Tell a story	7. Tell a personal anecdote
3. Find a quotation	8. Use humor
4. Use a visual aid	9. Reference expert opinion
5. Cite a statistic	10. Tell a success story

Figure 7.2 Ten techniques for making a powerful introduction

into the material? Dozens? Hundreds? Thousands? For us, it's been in the high hundreds, for sure. By this point in our lives, the lazy introduction is the quickest way to make us grab our iPads and start updating our Facebook pages or checking our various email accounts. We simply believe if you do not care enough to make a compelling introduction that captures our attention, we do not care enough to leave our iPads alone. The tips that follow, and in Figure 7.2, will help you supercharge your introduction and capture your audience's attention.

Don't limit yourself to using only one of the tips. Many introductions will use more than one of these tips:

Ask a Question

We like this approach least, because it's easy, but it is certainly better than no introduction at all. If you take this approach, make your question rhetorical or provocative. Anticipate the response you will get from the audience. We have seen too many presentations fall apart because the speaker asked a question and the audience didn't provide a response.

Tell a Story

We find stories about something you've read or something you've seen or someone you've known to be highly effective. Just make sure the story relates clearly to your topic. Stories not only engage your audience, but you can leave them with a cliffhanger you will return to in the presentation's conclusion.

Find a Quotation

We regularly thumb through online books of quotations when looking for ways to make compelling points. We figure if someone else has said it, and it's good enough to be in a book of quotations, then it's good enough for us. Plus, quotations make you look smart. Be sure to make the connection between your quote and the presentation's topic for your audience. You can even share a quotation and ask your audience questions about it if that works for you. We once delivered a presentation for a client about strategic planning. In an earlier chapter, we shared the following quote that is attributed to Dwight Eisenhower. We believe it is worth repeating: "Plans are nothing; planning is everything." We asked our audience to tell us what that meant in relation to their organization's strategic planning.

Use a Visual Aid

One of us once saw a politician begin a speech by holding up a gigantic screw made of Styrofoam and painted gold. It won't tax your imagination too much to learn that the politician was making a speech about government waste and the need to reduce taxes.

Cite a Statistic

We like Mark Twain's famous statement, "There are three types of lies—lies, damned lies, and statistics." Whether you agree with the author or not, a statistic can make a powerful point. Using statistics can be difficult because the data must really have a "wow factor." It must be truly jaw-dropping. The statistics also need to be relevant and accessible. In other words, people don't easily grasp large numbers. What do "a million smokers" look like? How large is a stack of "a trillion dollars?" It isn't really startling or dramatic if the statistic is not relevant and accessible.

Make a Startling Statement

We like these statements because they can be disruptive, provocative, or invoke laughter. There's hardly a better way to get someone's attention. Sarah Kay, the founder of Project V.O.I.C.E., delivered a now famous TED Talk. The presentation was about her work with Project V.O.I.C.E. teaching kids about the power of self-expression through spoken word poetry.[3] She said, "If I should have a daughter, instead of mom, she's gonna call me Point B, because that way she knows that no matter what happens, she can always find her way to me." These were the first words out of her mouth, and they had a profound impact on her audience. Watch her TED Talk here: http://www.ted.com/playlists/77/new_to_ted.html.

Tell a Personal Anecdote or Relay an Experience

We like these because stories are how people learn. It's the reason we've included so many in our book.

Use Humor

We like a good joke. But, we caution you to be very careful with humor. What one person laughs at, another finds incredibly offensive. Save your best retelling of Chris Rock jokes for your bar buddies.

Reference Expert Opinion

We like using expert opinions because it is a way to build credibility.

Tell a Success Story

We Americans love success, almost as much as we like to see successful people fail and come back from their failures. And remember, you can always use hypothetical stories, as long as that is clear with your audience.

Maximizing Your Impact

Having a supercharged introduction should get your audience engaged in your presentation. However, as we can tell you from years of experience in the classroom, getting an audience's attention and keeping it are two different things. As speakers, we need to work to keep our audience plugged in during the heart of the presentation as well. Figure 7.3 summarizes 11 ideas for keeping your audience engaged and maximizing your impact during a presentation.

1. Remember that you are the presentation	6. Show your resilience
2. Look your best	7. Do not memorize
3. Put a smile on your face	8. Demonstrate your magnetism
4. Demonstrate your passion	9. Create potential
5. Explain your purpose, then repeat and repeat again	10. Empower your audience
	11. Believe in yourself

Figure 7.3 Tips for maximizing your impact

Consider how you can apply the 11 tips to improve your presentation impact:

- *Remember that YOU are the presentation.* Slides, handouts, leave-behinds, and other visual aids are awesome, but they aren't the presentation, YOU are.
- *Look your best—your very best.* People say don't judge a book by its cover, but we all do it to some degree. In fact, some research suggests that "humans can categorize others in less than 150 milliseconds."[4]
- *Put a smile on your face.* People who smile when they speak automatically "sound" more cheerful, warm, and approachable. Emotions, after all, are contagious.[5]
- *Demonstrate your passion.* If you don't show a metaphorical fire for your topic, your audience surely won't be inspired to listen and later recall your message.
- *Explain your purpose, then repeat and repeat again.* From the get-go, tell your audience what you want them to remember from your presentation. In your main points, reinforce what you want them to remember from your presentation. Then, when concluding, remind them again what you want them to remember.
- *Show your resilience.* Don't let interruptions such as questions from the audience rattle your nerves. Know your material well enough to answer questions. During a group presentation, be able to answer generally a question that might best be handled by someone else, and then hand off that question to the appropriate teammate for a more detailed response. Then, be prepared to pick back up where you left off.

- **Do NOT memorize.** Memorization prevents you from accomplishing number 6 above. Further, if you falter, it is very difficult to recover if you have memorized a presentation. Finally, if you memorize, you are less likely to sound conversational.
- **Demonstrate your magnetism.** The ability to attract money, people, and ideas is powerful, and it also helps your credibility.
- **Create potential.** Show your audience what is possible. They need to see the world you envision. Demonstrate the now versus the future.
- **Empower your audience.** Show your audience how their actions can have profoundly positive consequences. Give them the tools and guidance they need to carry out your ideas.
- **Believe in yourself.** Perfect practice makes perfect performance. Any athlete who is any good at his or her sport is an athlete who has done the same things over and over again, perhaps thousands of times. When you put that level of effort into your presentation, just like the athlete, you can't help but be confident.

Closing Well

You've heard them before: highly paid, very influential people ending a presentation or speech with "thank you" or "are there any questions" or, if he or she is a politician, "God bless America." Well, just because people use these closers doesn't mean these are good closing statements. It's just like when you were a child and you wanted to do something that your mother or father wouldn't allow. You might have whined, "But everyone else is doing it." And your parent(s) may have responded, "If everyone else were eating worms would you want them for dinner?" We hope you answered no. So if all these important people end their presentations with weak closing statements like the ones mentioned before, why do they do it? There are at least two reasons. First, it's not offensive. Second, it's easy.

By now, however, you've probably come to realize that we aren't big proponents of easy. This entire chapter attempts to persuade you to make

1. If you told a story at the beginning of the presentation, return to that story and tie it to the major point(s) you want your audience to remember.
2. Find a short verse that refers to the beginning of your presentation and that gains the audience's attention through humor, empathy, sympathy, or inspiration.
3. Find a short quote from a famous person that reinforces the major points of your presentation.
4. Give a signal that you are closing. For example, "To recap the major points of my presentation, I ask you to remember. . . " or "In conclusion, please remember. . ."
5. Deliver a call to action. For example, "I challenge you to. . . " or "Join me in . . . " makes it easy for people to comply with your requests and ask them to respond quickly. The greater the distance between your request and the audience's action, the more likely they are to do nothing.

Figure 7.4 Tips for delivering a memorable closing

a *memorable* presentation—one that the audience will recall and be influenced by well after you leave the stage, dais, or lectern. In our classes, we have adopted harsh penalties for student presentations that end in the expected way of "thank you" or "are there any questions." We encourage our students, and we encourage you, to push the limits of your comfort zone to develop memorable closing statements that summarize your major points (telling the audience what you've already told them) and reference the beginning of your presentation (tying the bow on top of the gift-wrapped box). The tips in Figure 7.4 are just a few of the many ways you can deliver a memorable closing.

Achieving Conversational Delivery Style

Search your memories for the most boring lecture, sermon, speech, or presentation you ever heard. We're willing to bet that one of the reasons you found it boring was the speaker didn't present in a conversational style. Public speaking blogger Olivia Mitchell and researchers Mayer, Fennell, Farmer, and Campbell (2004) agree that a conversational style, rather than a formal style, helps people learn better.[6] The late Steve Jobs, co-founder of Apple Computers, was very nearly a genius at presenting in a conversational style. We've considered the effectiveness of three additional individuals who are typically believed to have been great 20th and 21st century communicators and have gleaned tips from their style to share with you. Our tips are based on the speaking success of Jobs, the Rev. Billy Graham, President Barack Obama, and the late President Ronald Reagan. The lessons have been packaged into the six simple ideas in Figure 7.5 that anyone can use.

1. When writing your script, imagine you are writing to one person and one person only. When proofreading your script, put the words "Hey, Joe" or "Hey, Jane" before a sentence and read it aloud to yourself. Does it sound like you're speaking to a friend?

2. When rehearsing your delivery, imagine you are speaking directly to one person and one person only. Even if your audience has thousands of people in it, you still must reach one person at a time.

3. When presenting, avoid looking at your screen if you are using one for projecting images. Rather, look at one person at a time in your audience and speak directly to him or her. If you wish, glance at your screen or gesture to it, but never speak to it.

4. When writing, and later when presenting, seek ways to connect emotionally with your audience.

5. When rehearsing, imagine the one person in your audience who will be the most difficult to reach. Spend extra time figuring out how best to reach that one hard-to-reach person (in marketing terms, this person is your target).

6. When speaking, get out from behind the lectern. How many dinner conversations have you had from behind a lectern?

Figure 7.5 *Tips for achieving conversational delivery style*

Designing Slides and Decks for Memorable Presentations

Please don't tell Bill Gates, but we really hate Microsoft's PowerPoint software. It isn't that the product is bad. It's that the product is awful. PowerPoint has allowed people with little or no graphic design taste to create slide presentations. These presentations are sometimes referred to as "decks." Many professors and other professionals rely entirely too much on slides. How so? They simply read what is on their slides (or decks). For these situations we borrow the term "death by PowerPoint," because it describes how these excruciatingly mundane presentations bore people to death. In this section, we will give you a few pieces of simple advice that will eliminate most of the errors that create "death by PowerPoint." For a detailed treatment of slide and deck design, we recommend the work of Garr Reynolds, who wrote *Presentation Zen*, which outlines an approach where less, much less, is more.[7] If you are a nondesigner like us, then you will also find Robin Williams' book, *The Non-Designer's Design Book*, to be useful.[8]

Consider the slide in Figure 7.6. It breaks the one rule you should always follow in slide design: You are the presentation! The slides should reinforce your message, not hijack it. If your audience can read your slides, then they have no use for you.

How did the presenter end up with such a wordy slide? The main culprit is sloth. PowerPoint and similar programs are designed with default

---

Who's Protecting the Children?

- Senator Charles Schumer of New York proposed banning the suspect baby bottles outright.
- Wal-Mart, Toys "R" Us, and CVS all announced plans to phase out polycarbonate bottles. Some companies have adopted BPA-free plastic.
- Yet most businesses stuck with BPA products -- at least partly because they don't have a good substitute. Nearly all of the 130 billion food and beverage cans made in the United States each year are still lined with a BPA resin. The alternative called Oleoresin, is more expensive, has a shorter shelf life, and can't be used for acidic foods like tomatoes.
- Senator Frank Lautenberg of New Jersey has proposed an overhaul of the whole system. In May 2008, he introduced the Kid-Safe Chemical Act. The Act would reverse the burden of proof on chemicals, requiring manufacturers to demonstrate their safety in order to keep them in commerce. The E.U. passed a similar law in 2006, as did Canada in 1999. (Canada has banned BPA in baby bottles.)
- The National Toxicology Program advised "concerned parents" to reduce their use of canned foods; use BPA-free baby bottles; and opt for glass, porcelain, or stainless-steel containers, particularly for hot foods and liquids.

Figure 7.6 Wordy slide

settings. When you open up a blank presentation and begin working with a slide, the bullet points are right there for you to use. How convenient. Are we wrong, or are we not sentient beings? Just because a program is set up with defaults, we are not compelled to use the defaults. Instead, we encourage you to figure out the point of each slide and to draw by hand—don't worry, we use stick figures—what you want the slide to look like. Alternatively, you can think about images that might evoke an emotional connection to the topic at hand. Once you're satisfied, open PowerPoint and try to force the program to recreate the drawing for you, or insert the image for you.

In Figure 7.7, we revised the slide from Figure 7.6. Less is more. The slide in Figure 7.7 would make an emotional connection with any audience. The audience would much rather look at a picture of an adorable baby and listen to you provide the details. What they would dislike is listening to you read the content from the slide in Figure 7.6.

Audiences don't just dislike wordy slides; they also dislike slides with tables and graphs that have too much information. The audience cannot reasonably process complex tables and graphs and listen to you. Again, if you remember that you are the message, you will limit your tables and graphs to images that can be processed quickly so your audience

Figure 7.7 Revised wordy slide

will focus on what you are saying. This approach to slide design requires you to be more thoughtful about your presentation materials, but with thoughtfulness and hard work, you won't victimize your audience.

Putting It All Together

We realized people would find it helpful if we could create a set of tips that help bring together the utmost important points regarding making memorable presentations. Consequently, we developed the tips below. Initially, we used these tips for a professional development activity we conducted three consecutive years for the *Travelers EDGE* program. We liked the tips so much that we now share them with all our students. Funny enough, we can always tell which students follow these tips, and which do not. Even more funny, the students are always astounded that we can tell the difference. Those wacky students.

Conclusion

By now, we hope to have persuaded you that you MUST give a memorable presentation. Through our examples and anecdotes, as well as our lists of tips, we have equipped you with the tools you need to give a memorable presentation and wallop your competition. Because most people present so poorly, when you present memorably you create a professional brand identity for yourself that sets you far apart from others. We have seen time and again, regardless of industry, that the professionals who present in a polished and memorable manner are the professionals who advance in their careers.

Ten Great Ideas for Fantastic Presentations

1. Start with an outline.
   - Write an outline of what you want to cover.
   - Develop three to five major points you want your audience to remember.
   - Remember that less is more. So, don't tell the audience too much.
   - Don't bore the audience.
   - Give your presentation a strong beginning, middle, and end.
   - Build slides from your outline.
   - Avoid Microsoft templates. People have seen them to the point of boredom. Same goes for Apple/Macintosh. (Note: This rule may be violated if you work for an organization that requires all presentations to follow a common format or template.)
2. Tell them one thing at a time.
   - Cover only one main idea per slide.
   - Limit sub points to three and show them as bullets.
   - Use no animation to introduce the bullets or the topics.
   - Introduce all bullets at the same time, unless you are very skillful at using a remote, wireless mouse device for "clicking" through the bullets.
3. Display no paragraphs.
   - Remember a picture is worth a thousand words.
   - Remember paragraphs can get you arrested for murder: murder by PowerPoint.
   - Your slides are the *illustrations* for your presentation, *not* the presentation itself.
4. Design for design's sake is a mistake.
   - Remember that simplicity is not boring.
   - Use dark type on light backgrounds or white type on dark backgrounds.
   - Clip art, animated fades, swipes, flashing text, and other gimmicks are annoying.
   - Use sans-serif fonts such as Arial, Helvetica, or Calibri for headlines.

- Use serif fonts such as Times New Roman or Garamond for body.
- Use no more than two fonts.
- Limit use of bold, underline, and italic fonts.
- Use left-justified or right-justified text. Centered text is harder to read and looks like a party invitation.
- Avoid placing type on top of a photo, unless the photo is screened way back (25% transparent).

5. Use images to tell your story.
   - Find beautiful photographs or images to illustrate your point, and talk to your audience about how the image makes your point.
   - Avoid clip art.
   - Use clean, easy-to-read charts and graphs.
   - Make sure numbers on charts and graphs are readable from the back of the room.

6. Slides are not the presentation—YOU ARE!
   - Remember that slides are a small part of your presentation.
   - Polish your part of the presentation—your attire, your grooming, your posture, your voice, your diction, your eye contact with your audience.
   - Remember that people are expecting you to convey your message.
   - Remember not to look back at your slides.
   - Remember that NO ONE wants to hear you read.

7. Get their attention immediately.
   - Remember that your presentation needs to gain the audience's attention, just like a song, a movie, a book, or a TV program has to grab the audience's attention immediately.
   - Start with something other than introducing yourself.
   - Start with a story, anecdote, or quote that is appropriate to your topic. For example: "Let me tell you a story" will almost always make an audience sit up and take notice.
   - Appeal to your audience's emotions, if possible.

8. Ask questions, maybe.

- Using a question-and-answer period is often effective. It is not, however, a good conclusion to your presentation. "Are there any questions?" is not enough to announce the conclusion of your presentation.
- Using a strong conclusion, then transitioning to a question-and-answer session can be effective. For example, if you started with a story to get your audience's attention, return to that story to conclude your presentation. Then announce, "Now that I've reached the end of my presentation, I'm happy to answer questions that popped into your mind while I was presenting." Or, you might try this: "You've been a great, attentive audience. Now, why don't you tell me what you thought? Who has comments or questions?"

9. Practice, practice, practice.
   - Practice your presentation before a friend or family member whom you trust to tell you what you NEED to hear, not what you WANT to hear.
   - Record your presentation practice session with a video camera, camera phone, or other technology. Critique yourself, looking for ways to polish and improve.
   - Practice your presentation even if you've given it before. It's easy to get lazy and fall into traps by being overly confident.
   - Practice in the location where you are scheduled to present, if possible.
   - Know the layout of the room where you will present.
   - Do not fall into a drone, going on and on and on and on and on with only minimal changes to your inflection.
   - Do not ramble.
   - Always present as if you were talking with someone you know, not as if you were reading off notes.

10. Plan, plan, plan.
    - Arrive early the day of the presentation.
    - Test the equipment in the room before your presentation, if at all possible.

- Assume nothing—check in advance whether you'll be using a computer on sight that has Windows 7 or Windows 98, Microsoft Office 2010 or 2007. It is your responsibility to make sure your technology is compatible with the technology you'll use.
- Do not use YouTube. If you want to use video, import it into your presentation as a video clip, not as a hypertext link.
- Cue up your digital or analog media, such as a DVD, CD, or videotape to make sure these don't create a problem or a distraction in your presentation.
- Have a back-up plan (or two) in case your technology fails. For example, have your presentation on two different jump drives (thumb drives) in case one fails; and, have printouts of your slides with you in case the technology fails.
- Remind yourself continuously what it is you hope your audience remembers after your presentation. Stay on message.

CHAPTER 8

Why Must I Know How to Influence and Persuade Others?

After a long career in marketing communications and public relations, Robert has learned that influence can be hard to exert, but when done so properly has wide-ranging impact. One memorable experience he had while working for the Independent Bankers Association of America (IBAA) in the middle 1990s, was trying to influence public opinion regarding ATM fees. Robert turned to the media, helping to place bankers on financial news programs and being interviewed himself by National Public Radio's Jim Zarolli.

The message that IBAA was sending to the public, through the media, was that small, independent banks didn't gouge customers on ATM fees the way the megabanks did. The wire services and CNN picked up the story, and soon there were articles appearing in papers across the United States, and on the web, that gave IBAA's message in clear, consumer-friendly terms. Almost 20 years later, bank fees are still a bone of contention for consumers, and a tremendous source of revenue for the big banks.

Not all messages of influence or persuasion are directed at large audiences. In fact, both of us believe that most messages sent in a business setting contain some element of influence or persuasion. While we haven't conducted an empirical study on the matter, our collective experiences have led us to that conclusion. Many times our efforts to influence or persuade are one-on-one or one-to-a-few tasks.

Consider this example: If you are sending an email to a client with a status report on a project, you are attempting to influence the receiver of the message in a positive way to convey your competence and capability, as well as maintain a good relationship with him or her. Further, if you are sending a transmittal memo with a quarterly earnings report to the C-level managers, you are attempting to influence those senior executives in such a way as they can trust the accuracy of your numbers.

Since the days of the Classical Greek and Roman scholars, people have been interested in the most effective ways to persuade and influence others. Therefore, there is no surprise that scholars today are still studying the topics, while practitioners employ various techniques to influence or persuade. Before we delve into theory and techniques, let's spend a moment reflecting on the meaning of persuasion and influence. In this chapter, you'll notice that we use influence and persuasion interchangeably, but that approach lacks a certain amount of precision.

Merriam-Webster's online dictionary provides this definition of influence: *the power or capacity of causing an effect in indirect or intangible ways*. It gives the following definition for persuasion: *the act or process or an instance of persuading*; and, finally, defines persuasion as *to move by argument, entreaty, or expostulation to a belief, position or course of action*. You can see that influence and persuasion are related much as a mother is related to her child.

While we mentioned the Classical Greeks and Romans who studied persuasion, we won't spend time rehashing ancient history. However, one contemporary model of persuasion comes to us from Petty and Cacioppo's[1] Elaboration Likelihood Model (ELM). The reason we mention this model is, in part, because it has been broadly and frequently used in empirical research studies across several disciplines, including communication and psychology.

At its most basic, the ELM demonstrates (see Figure 8.1) that there are two routes to persuasion through argumentation: central and peripheral. The central route requires substantial cognitive processing, what we might call careful thought. You could think of it as a more data-driven approach. A strong argument, backed up with strong evidence—numbers for example—should lead to a stronger persuasive effect. The peripheral route requires less cognitive, careful thought. You might think of it as an emotionally driven approach. A beautiful person, presenting a weak argument—without any evidence for example—should lead to a weaker persuasive effect. Believe it or not, research indicates that beautiful people

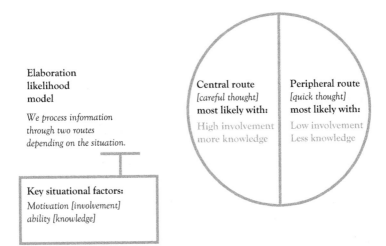

Figure 8.1 Elaboration likelihood model

are more influential because their appearance attracts the attention of others. Notice also in the graphic that there are situational factors, motivation/involvement, and ability/knowledge that are part of the ELM. High involvement/motivation might be a person's interest in stopping a behavior that causes negative health outcomes, for example, binge drinking. Low involvement/less knowledge could be a person's interest in attending a cultural event, a poetry reading for example.

Now, the ELM doesn't suggest that just because you are beautiful you will be persuasive, but it will help you get someone's attention. But how can we apply the ELM in business communication, you might wonder? Easy. Let's say you need to gain an employee's attention and deliver the message that his consistent tardiness is negatively impacting business operations. This message is one the employee would not wish to receive, plus it's one that you hope will cause the individual to come to work on time.

Using the peripheral route, you might first gain his attention through the careful use of humor, to establish likability. Or you might use an incentive—such as lunch, which is relatively low involvement—to get that person to have positive feelings about the meeting. Using the central route, you lay out the dispassionate details of the person's tardiness. You might, for example, indicate the precise number of times the employee was late in a pay period, and by how many minutes. You provide a precise calculation of how much money that has cost the individual. Then, you comment that you know the employee is a good person and a good worker who would never steal from the firm. Yet, habitual tardiness has the net impact of actually stealing from the organization—which is relatively high involvement.

Petty and Cacioppo's ELM explains that persuasion exists on a continuum. In the example we provide above, we are looking at using both routes to persuasion with an ultimate outcome of strong persuasion and substantial behavioral change (i.e., stop coming to work late!).

When audiences evaluate persuasive appeals, they process information simultaneously about both the sender of that appeal and the appeal itself. The theories driving research in this area have substantial range when it comes to their complexity. When it comes to persuasion and influence, we don't want to confuse you; we prefer to keep it simple. Therefore, in this chapter, we will share with you some simple ideas to keep in mind when making any type of persuasive appeal.

How People Learn Our Persuasive Messages

We have come to appreciate the simplicity and effectiveness of what is known as message learning theory. Message learning theory is the result of research conducted by researchers at Yale in the 1940s and 1950s under the direction of Carl Hovland. The theory argues that when processing information about a persuasive message, audience members have to go through a series of steps before real attitude change will occur. The steps, identified in Figure 8.2 below, suggest that for persuasive messages to be effective, they must capture the audience's attention, be comprehensible, and cause the audience members to yield to and retain the message's information.[2]

The takeaways from message learning are clear. To improve your odds at persuading or influencing others, you must present them with messages that capture their attention, make the information easy to understand,

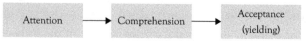

Figure 8.2 Message learning process

and help audience members retain the information for recall. So how can we apply these ideas to our business communications?

Step 1 suggests that we need to get our audience's attention. If you recall, in Chapter 7, we provided you with a number of ways to supercharge your presentation introductions (e.g., telling stories, sharing statistics, and using humor). We gave you that advice because we know that these are ways to get people to focus on your message, to engage them right from the beginning. Message learning theory supports that basic approach.

Step 2 suggests that our persuasive messages must be comprehensible, or easy to understand. We can accomplish this through a variety of means. For example, Robert's story near the beginning of this chapter about banking ATM fees is a fine example of enhancing audience comprehension. He mentioned writing a press release that included consumer-friendly terms. The words we use go a long way toward helping our audiences understand information. Organizing information for audience members is another way that we make it easier for them to understand the information. It is also important for us to understand and meet our audience's information needs.

Step 3 suggests that persuasive messages must be easy to recall. How can we enhance recall? We have many tactics at our disposal, but here are a few examples:

- Repeat important pieces of information.
- Provide information in small, digestible chunks.
- Employ mnemonic devices.
- Tie your message to something personally or professionally relevant to your audience.
- Reduce or eliminate distractions from the message.

Our list is by no means exhaustive, but it should give you a good starting point. Some research suggests—and rightly so—that simply retaining information will not make that information more persuasive.[3] In fact, there are many factors that influence actual attitude and behavior change. Perhaps most important is that not all people respond to information in the same way. An argument that is persuasive to one person may not have the same affect on another person. As always with communication, the more you know about your audience, the better able you will be to achieve your message's strategic objectives.

How People Process Information About You

As we said previously, when confronted by persuasive messages, people process information about both the message and its sender. This should make sense because we all know that messages are not processed in a vacuum. Although we know that people we may think of as "crackpots," "know nothings," or "do littles," can occasionally have brilliant ideas, we are less likely to believe them when they share those ideas. These people aren't terribly convincing because we have a difficult time separating our thoughts about the message from our thoughts about the sender. This failure is a fallacy that audiences make called the genetic fallacy, where we believe the origin of an idea affects its quality. Research tells us that what seems to matter most when people are processing information about the senders of persuasive appeals are credibility and likability.[4]

Let's consider credibility. In Chapter 1, we shared with you our conclusion that your credibility drives your effectiveness. In that chapter, we discussed that credibility comprises your trustworthiness (warmth) and expertise (strength). A recent article in *Harvard Business Review* described the significance of these two traits.

> Why are these traits so important? Because they answer two critical questions: "What are this person's intentions toward me?" and "Is he or she capable of acting on those intentions?" Together these assessments underlie our emotional and behavioral reactions to other people, groups, and even brands and companies.[5]

Those professionals with the most persuasive power are thought to have both trustworthiness and expertise. The tricky thing about these traits is that they are, what social scientists call, perceiver constructs. In other words, nobody possesses credibility. Instead, a person's credibility exists entirely in the mind of the perceiver (i.e., the audience). Therefore, we are only as credible as our audience believes us to be. All of this must beg the question, How can we get others to perceive us as trustworthy experts?

Think about those people in your professional world who you consider to be highly trustworthy. How did those people make that impression on you? Our guess is that the people you are thinking about are trustworthy because they deliver on their promises, they have provided you with help when they didn't have to, they found ways to connect you to people who would be good for your career, they took the time to see the world from your perspective, or all. Ultimately, people who are trustworthy can be relied upon and demonstrate goodwill by considering your needs and well-being. If you want to be more persuasive, then you should look to others whom you consider trustworthy and model your behavior after those people. Here are a few other things you can do to enhance your trustworthiness:[6]

- Share personal stories (when appropriate) to show that you can trust others enough to confide in them.
- Confirm others' feelings in a way that demonstrates that you understand their perspective.
- Work to establish common ground with others.
- Be sincere and authentic.

The other side of the credibility coin is expertise. It is important that you demonstrate to others that you are an expert in your area. When Jason talks to his class about expertise, he asks his students, "Who is the communication expert in the room, and how do you know that?" Typically, at least one of the students will speak up quickly and say, "You are because you told us about your education and work." If you want to have influence over others, you should let them know that you are the expert to whom they should listen. In Chapter 1, we told you about impression management. You have some degree of control over how people think of you. In addition to simply telling others about your expertise and developing a reputation as an expert, you can use your knowledge to gain influence at work in other ways. Recent research suggests that you can use your expertise to (a) create a means for helping key decision makers evaluate complex information in your area of expertise, (b) share information with other experts while learning from their expertise, and (c) help others interpret the results of complex information.[7]

Cialdini's Principles of Influence[8]

Now that you have a better understanding of how audiences evaluate you and your persuasive appeals, let's turn our attention to specific tactics that you can use to enhance your attempts at persuasion and influence. To do so, we rely heavily on the work of marketing and influence guru Dr. Robert Cialdini, whose work on influence has resulted in what he calls the six principles of influence. Those principles are commitment/consistency, authority, liking, reciprocity, scarcity, and social proof. Let's look at each principle and how they have been used.

Commitment/Consistency

This principle suggests that people have a need to be consistent. When people make a commitment to do something, or when they publicly express a particular set of values, they will be more likely to act consistently with those commitments. For example, Jason lost some weight a couple of years ago by using the Weight Watchers diet. The diet has no mystery—eat fewer calories and you will lose weight. Jason understands that basic idea, but why was the diet effective? It was effective because Jason made a public commitment to lose weight and was held publicly accountable through meetings. This principle tells us that if we can get others to make commitments publicly, they will work to behave in line with those commitments.

If you listen to public radio, then you are familiar with their pledge campaigns. One way that our local station uses this principle is by telling listeners that they share the station's values. They will begin pitches by saying things like, "We know that you value public radio. We know that you share our love of objective journalism that is free from corporate influence. You share our desire for truth in reporting. We know that you are committed to keeping public radio alive." The radio station is using commitment to set the stage for asking for a donation. Listeners are left with the choice of agreeing with the statement and making a contribution, agreeing with the statement and making no contribution, or disagreeing with the statement and making a decision about the contribution. Those who agree and really care will be more likely to respond favorably to the appeal.

Authority

The authority principle suggests that people tend to defer to those with expertise. Stanley Milgram demonstrated this principle through his classic experiments in which subjects continued to deliver what they believed to be electrical shocks to others simply because a researcher in a lab coat instructed them to do so. Don't worry. No real shocks were ever delivered. The studies are fascinating and still controversial.[9] If you followed our advice above, then you should have greater influence. If you are not the recognized expert on a particular topic, you should enlist the help of those who are thought to be experts.

Liking

The liking principle is simple. People are more likely to say yes to requests from people they like. Jason's pantry shelf holds evidence of this principle. His wife has been invited by a friend to Pampered Chef parties. His wife, because she likes her friend, feels a sense of obligation to the friend and purchases boxes of cooking utensils that now collect dust in the pantry. The best way to enhance your liking is to demonstrate similarities that you have with your audience. In the social media age, the power of liking as a tool of influence may become more prominent. We have the power to turn to our social networks for information and advice, even when it isn't solicited.

Reciprocity

The reciprocity principle suggests that people return favors. When you help others, they are more likely to help you when you need it. In a recent interview, Cialdini said, "Get in the habit of helping people out, and don't wave it away and say, 'Oh, no big deal.' We have serious persuasive power immediately after someone thanks us."[10] We see reciprocity as the foundation of professional networking, and it just happens to be a powerful tool of influence.

Scarcity

The scarcity principle suggests that people place tremendous value on things that they believe to be in short supply. You need not look much farther than your local jewelry store to see this principle in practice. Those diamonds come with a high price tag and may not be as rare as you think. In our communications, we can enhance scarcity by reminding people of what they stand to lose if they do not take our recommendations.

Social Proof

The social proof principle suggests that when people are in unfamiliar situations, or don't know what to do, they will look to what others are doing. No doubt you've heard the expression *when in Rome.* If you want people to behave in certain ways, then you should demonstrate how others are doing so. To enhance the influence of social proof, you need to demonstrate how those "others" are similar to the target of your persuasive appeal. We published a study recently that demonstrated how social proof could be used to reduce student absenteeism in college classrooms. In the study, we presented students with a course absenteeism policy that provided actual absenteeism data from students "just like you." Students were not rewarded or punished for attendance or absenteeism; they were simply told how many classes the typical A, B, C, D, and F students had missed in the past. Students who were given social proof, missed fewer classes than those students who did not receive social proof.[11]

Conclusion

This chapter provided you with the nuts and bolts of persuasion and influence. The lessons of this chapter are clear. To be highly influential, you should

- put your audience first;
- craft messages that are learnable;
- pay attention to your personal credibility;
- use the appropriate tactics for every situation.

Why must you know how to influence and persuade others? Because that is the route to success in the world of business, and communication is the tool we use to leverage our influence.

In the foreword for this book we made you a promise. We assured you that we weren't going to tell you that your current business communication is all wrong. We hope, however, that this book helps you learn how to improve your business communication and how important it is to make steady incremental progress in your growth as a business communicator. Many of us learn best through the use of metaphors and allegories. Consequently, what follows relies on metaphors and allegories to make clear our points about your growth as a business communicator.

One of us has run a marathon and the other taught yoga for a few years. We believe that you can take important lessons about business communication from our extracurricular activities. To complete a marathon, a runner must train for months—gradually increasing the distance traveled as well as the ability to push through discomfort. A marathon is allegorical to your progress toward the goal of exceptional business communication: it is a long-term commitment requiring a great deal of practice and preparation. Yoga practitioners understand that the mind and body are interconnected, and that the strengths and weaknesses of both must be recognized and respected. Yoga practice is allegorical to exceptional business communication in that both require us to recognize our strengths and weaknesses, positives and negatives, and to view our practice as a continuous journey toward something better, rather than a destination of perfection at which we arrive and remain.

Notes

Chapter 1

1. *Quotationsbook.com* (2013).
2. Kristafer (2013).
3. Berlo (1960).
4. Buck and VanLear (2002).
5. Mead (1963).
6. Rogers (1993).
7. Watzlawick, Beavin, and Jackson (1967).
8. Burgoon and Hale (1984).
9. Mehrabian (1972).
10. Neiva and Hickson III (2003).
11. Levine, Feeley, McCornack, Hughes, and Harms (2005).
12. Snyder and Lee-Partridge (2013).
13. Perez, Gorman, and Barrett (2012).
14. Klosowski (2012).
15. This section is based on Gambardella (2013).
16. Middleton (2011).
17. Garber (2013).
18. *The state of meetings today* (2013).
19. Merrill (2012).
20. Ferguson (2013).
21. Hamilton and Hunter (1998).
22. Priester and Petty (2003).
23. Witt Associates (2011).
24. Bolino, Varela, Bande, and Turnley (2006).
25. Holmes (2013).

Chapter 2

1. Cutteridge (2013).
2. D'Urso and Pierce (2009).
3. Lee-Partridge and Snyder (2012).
4. Gill (2013).
5. Purcell (2011).
6. Goleman (1995).

7. McDowell (1993).
8. Warrell (2012).
9. Siegel (Producer). (2006)
10. Snyder and Lee-Partridge (2013).
11. Duggan and Rainie (2012).
12. Facebook (2013).
13. Statistics Brain (2012).
14. YouTube (2013).
15. LinkedIn (2013).
16. Kazek (2013).
17. Shigley (2013).
18. Barnes, Lescault, and Andonian (2013).
19. Primack (2013).
20. Marsden (2010).
21. Southwest Airlines (2013).

Chapter 3

1. Canavor (2012).
2. Guffey and Loewy (2012).
3. Kirsch, Jungeblut, Jenkins, and Kolstad (1993).
4. Guffey and Loewy (2012).
5. Miller (1956).

Chapter 4

1. Weir (2013).
2. Oxford Dictionary Online (2013).
3. Wilson (2013).

Chapter 5

1. Kotz (2013).
2. Bodell (2012).

Chapter 6

1. Dunn and Smith (2011).
2. Dunn and Smith (2011).

3. This section is based on Grinols (2010a).
4. Grinols (2010b).
5. Hokunson III (2013).
6. Weir (2013).

Chapter 7

1. Norem (2001).
2. Duarte (2012).
3. Project V.O.I.C.E. (2013).
4. Elsbach (2003).
5. Hatfield, Cacioppo, and Rapson (1993).
6. Mayer, Fennell, Farmer, and Campbell (2004).
7. Reynolds (2012).
8. Williams (2004).

Chapter 8

1. Petty and Cacioppo (1986).
2. Hovland, Janis, and Kelly (1953).
3. Eagly and Chaiken (1993).
4. Hamilton and Mineo (1996); Petty and Cacioppo (1986).
5. Cuddy, Kohut, and Neffinger (2013).
6. Cuddy et al. (2013).
7. Mikes, Hall, and Millo (2013).
8. This section is based on Cialdini (2007).
9. Shermer (2012).
10. Cliffe (2013).
11. Snyder, Forbus, and Cistulli (2012).

References

Barnes, N. G., Lescault, A. M., & Andonian, J. (2013). *Social media surge by the 2012 Fortune 500: Increase use of blogs, Facebook, Twitter and more.* Retrieved February 10, 2013, from University of Massachusetts Dartmouth: http://www.umassd.edu/cmr/socialmedia/2012fortune500/

Berlo, D. (1960). *The process of communication: An introduction to theory and practice.* New York, NY: Holt, Reinhart, and Winston.

Bodell, L. (2012). *5 ways process is killing your productivity.* Retrieved July 2, 2013, from Fast Company: http://www.fastcompany.com/1837301/5-ways-process-killing-your-productivity

Bolino, M. C., Varela, J. A., Bande, B., & Turnley, W. H. (2006). The impact of impression-management tactics on supervisor ratings of organizational citizenship behavior. *Journal of Organizational Behavior 27*(3), 281–297.

Buck, R., & VanLear, C. A. (2002). Verbal and nonverbal communication: Distinguishing symbolic, spontaneous, and pseudo-spontaneous nonverbal behavior. *Journal of Communication 52*(3), 522–541.

Burgoon, J., & Hale, J. (1984). The fundamental topoi of relational communication. *Communication Monographs 51*(3), 193–214.

Canavor, N. (2012). *Business writing in the digital age.* Thousand Oaks, CA: Sage.

Cialdini, R. (2007). *Influence: The psychology of persuasion.* New York, NY: William Morrow and Company.

Cliffe, S. (2013, July–August). Spotlight: Interview with Robert Cialdini. *Harvard Business Review,* 76–81.

Cuddy, A. J. C., Kohut, M., & Neffinger, J. (2013, July–August). Connect, then lead: To exert influence, you must balance competence and warmth. *Harvard Business Review,* 55–61.

D'Urso, S., & Pierce, K. M. (2009). Connected to the organization: A survey of communication technologies in the modern organizational landscape. *Communication Research Reports 26*(1), 75–81.

Duarte, N. (2012). *Persuasive presentations: Inspire action, engage the audience, sell your ideas.* Cambridge, MA: Harvard Business Review Press.

Duggan, M., & Rainie, L. (2012). *Cell phone activities 2012.* Retrieved March 15, 2013, from http://pewinternet.org/Reports/2012/Cell-Activities/Additional-Demographic-Analysis/Demographics.aspx

Dunn, T. N., & Smith, J. (2011). *Mr. Brown, listen to me…I know every injury that my child sustained. My son could have survived but he bled to death.* Retrieved

February 25, 2013, from The Sun: http://www.thesun.co.uk/sol/homepage/news/campaigns/our_boys/2722174/Jacqui-Janes-Mr-Brown-listen-to-me-My-son-could-have-survived-but-he-bled-to-death.html

Eagly, A. H., & Chaiken, S. (1993). *The psychology of attitudes*. Fort Worth, TX: Harcourt, Brace, & Janovich.

Elsbach, K. D. (2003). How to pitch a brilliant idea. In *HBR's 10 must reads on communication*. Cambridge, MA: Harvard Business Review Press.

Facebook. (2013). *Key facts*. Retrieved February 10, 2013, from http://newsroom.fb.com/Key-Facts

Garber, M. (2013). *You probably write a novel's worth of email every year*. Retrieved January 8, 2013, from The Atlantic: http://www.theatlantic.com/technology/archive/2013/01/you-probably-write-a-novels-worth-of-email-every-year/266942/

Gill, B. (2013). Vision statement: E-mail: Not dead, evolving. *Harvard Business Review*. Retrieved July 2, 2013, from http://hbr.org/2013/06/e-mail-not-dead-evolving/

Goleman, D. (1995). *Emotional intelligence: Why it can matter more than IQ*. New York, NY: Bantam.

Grinols, A. (2010a). *Don't ask people to drink your dirty water*. Presented at the 2010 Convention of the Association for Business Communication, Chicago, IL.

Grinols, A. (2010b). *The last lecture: 7 values of effective communicators*. Presented at the 2010 Convention of the Association for Business Communication, Chicago, IL.

Guffey, M. E., & Loewy, D. (2012). *Essentials of business communication*. Mason, OH: South-Western Cengage.

Hamilton, M. A., & Hunter, J. E. (1998). The effect of language intensity on receiver evaluations of message, source, and topic. In M. Allen & R. W. Preiss (Eds.), *Persuasion: Advances through meta-analysis* (pp. 99–138). Cresskill, NJ: Hampton Press.

Hamilton, M. A., & Mineo, P. J. (1996). Personality and persuasibility: Developing a multidimensional model of belief systems. *World Communication 24*, 1–16.

Hatfield, E., Cacioppo, J. T., & Rapson, R. L. (1993). Emotional contagion. *Current Directions in Psychological Science 2*, 96–99.

Holmes, L. (2013). *Lance Armstrong and the cheapening of indignation*. Retrieved January 15, 2013, from National Public Radio: http://www.npr.org/blogs/monkeysee/2013/01/15/169412502/lance-armstrong-and-the-cheapening-of-indignation

Hovland, C. I., Janis, I. L., & Kelley, H. H. (1953). *Communication and persuasion*. New Haven, CT: Yale University Press.

Kazek, K. (2013). *Just ask TV reporter Shea Allen: Social media's not so funny when it gets you fired.* Retrieved July 30, 2013, from Birmingham News: http://www.al.com/living/index.ssf/2013/07/just_ask_tv_reporter_shea_alle.html

Kirsch, I. S., Jungeblut, A., Jenkins, L., & Kolstad, A. (1993). *Adult literacy in America.* Washington, DC: National Center for Education Statistics, U. S. Department of Education.

Klosowski, T. (2012). *How CIA director David Petraeus's emails were traced (and how to protect yourself).* Retrieved February 15, 2013, Lifehacker: http://lifehacker.com/5960080/how-cia-director-david-petraeus-was-traced-through-email-and-how-to-keep-it-from-happening-to-you

Lee-Partridge, J., & Snyder, J. L. (2012). *Using the layered model to understand employee selection of information and communication channels for information and knowledge sharing in project teams.* Manuscript published in the Proceedings of the Conference on Information Systems Applied Research. Retrieved from http://proc.conisar.org/2012/index.html

Levine, T. R., Feeley, T. H., McCornack, S. A., Hughes, M., & Harms, C. M. (2005). Testing the effects of nonverbal behavior training on accuracy in deception detection with the inclusion of a bogus training control group. *Western Journal of Communication 69*(3), 203–217.

LinkedIn. (2013). *About LinkedIn.* Retrieved February 10, 2013, from http://press.linkedin.com/about

Marsden, P. (2010). *Walmart's group-buy app in Facebook: 10 ideas for competitors.* Retrieved April 15, 2013, from http://digitalinnovationtoday.com/walmarts-group-buy-app-in-facebook-10-ideas-for-competitors-screenshots/

Mayer, R. E., Fennell, S., Farmer, L., & Campbell, J. (2004). A personalization effect in multimedia learning: Students learn better when words are in conversational style rather than formal style. *Journal of Educational Psychology 96,* 389–395.

McDowell, S. (1993). *Email etiquette II: Why emoticons (and emotional cues) work.* Retrieved March 10, 2013, from 99u: http://99u.com/articles/6991/email-etiquette-ii-why-emoticons-and-emotional-cues-work

Mead, M. (1963). Socialization and enculturation. *Current Anthropology 4,* 182–188.

Mehrabian, A. (1972). *Nonverbal communication.* Chicago, IL: Aldine-Atherton.

Merrill, D. (2012). *Why multitasking doesn't work.* Retrieved February 10, 2013, from Forbes: http://www.forbes.com/sites/douglasmerrill/2012/08/17/why-multitasking-doesnt-work/

Middleton, D. (2011). *Students struggle for words: Business schools put more emphasis on writing amid employer complaints.* Retrieved February 12, 2013, from Wall Street Journal Online: http://online.wsj.com/article/SB10001424052748703409904576174651780110970.html

Mikes, A., Hall, M., & Millo, Y. (2013, July–August). How experts gain influence: To increase their impact, functional leaders should develop four specific competencies. *Harvard Business Review,* 71–75.

Miller, G. A. (1956). The magical number seven, plus or minus two: Some limits on our capacity for processing information. *Psychological Review 63,* 81–97.

Neiva, E., & Hickson III, M. (2003). Deception and honesty in animal and human communication: A new look at communicative interaction. *Journal of Intercultural Research 32*(1), 23–45.

Norem, J. (2001). *The positive power of negative thinking.* Cambridge, MA: Basic Books.

Oxford Dictionary Online. (2013). Retrieved June 10, 2013, from http://oxforddictionaries.com/us

Perez, E., Gorman, S., & Barrett, D. (2012). *FBI scrutinized on Petraeus.* Retrieved February 15, 2013, from Wall Street Journal Online: http://online.wsj.com/article/SB10001424127887324073504578113460852395852.html?mod=WSJ_hps_LEFTTopStories

Petty, R. E., & Cacioppo, J. T. (1986). Communication and persuasion: Central and peripheral routes to attitude change. New York, NY: Springer-Verlag.

Priester, J. R., & Petty, R. E. (2003). The influence of spokesperson trustworthiness on message elaboration, attitude strength, and advertising effectiveness. *Journal of Consumer Psychology 13,* 408–421.

Primack, D. (2013). *SEC's new social media policy falls short.* Retrieved April 15, 2013, from Fortune: http://finance.fortune.cnn.com/2013/04/02/secs-social-media-policy-falls-short/

Project V.O.I.C.E. (2013). Retrieved June 20, 2013, from http://www.project-voice.net/

Purcell, K. (2011). *Search and email still top the list of most popular online activities.* Retrieved July 30, 2013, from Pew Internet and American Life Project: http://www.pewinternet.org/Reports/2011/Search-and-email/Report.aspx

Quotationsbook.com (2013). Retrieved March 5, 2013, from http://quotationsbook.com/quote/16436/

Reynolds, G. (2012). *Presentation Zen: Simple ideas on presentation design and delivery.* Berkeley, CA: New Riders.

Shermer, M. (2012). *What Milgram's shock experiments really mean.* Retrieved June 30, 2013, from Scientific American: http://www.scientificamerican.com/article.cfm?id=what-milgrams-shock-experiments-really-mean

Shigley, K. (2013). *Five tips for using social media to advance your career.* Retrieved February 10, 2013, from Coca Cola Company: http://www.coca-colacompany.com/stories/five-tips-for-using-social-media-to-advance-your-career

Siegel, R. (Producer). (2006). *All things considered*. Retrieved February 15, 2013, from National Public Radio: http://www.npr.org/templates/story/story. php?storyId=6383383

Snyder, J. L., & Lee-Partridge, J. (2013). Understanding communication channel choice in team knowledge sharing. *Corporate Communications: An International Journal 18*(4), 417–431.

Snyder, J. L., Forbus, R. G., & Cistulli, M. D. (2012). Attendance policies, student attendance, and instructor verbal aggressiveness. *Journal of Education for Business 87*(3), 145–151.

Southwest Airlines. (2013). *Nuts about Southwest*. Retrieved April 15, 2013, from http://www.blogsouthwest.com

Statistics Brain. (2012). *Twitter statistics*. Retrieved February 10, 2013, from http://www.statisticbrain.com/twitter-statistics/

The state of meetings today. (2013). Retrieved February 10, 2013, from http:// www.effectivemeetings.com/meetingbasics/meetstate.asp

Warrell, M. (2012). *Hiding behind email? Four times you should never use email*. Retrieved March 10, 2013, from Forbes: http://www.forbes.com/sites/ margiewarrell/2012/08/27/do-you-hide-behind-email/

Watzlawick, P., Beavin, J., & Jackson, D. (1967). *Pragmatics of human communication: A study of interactional patterns, pathologies, and paradoxes*. New York, NY: Norton.

Williams, R. (2004). *The non-designer's presentation book*. Berkeley, CA: Peachpit Press.

Witt Associates. (2011). *Connecticut October 2011 snowstorm power restoration report*. Retrieved July 30, 2013, from http://www.ctmirror.com/sites/default/ files/documents/CTPowerRestorationReport20111201%20FINAL.pdf

YouTube. (2013). *Statistics*. Retrieved February 10, 2013, from http://www. youtube.com/yt/press/statistics.html

Index

OTHER TITLES IN THE CORPORATE COMMUNICATION COLLECTION

Debbie DuFrene, Stephen F. Austin State University, Editor

- *Managing Investor Relations: Strategies for Effective Communication* by Alexander Laskin
- *Managing Virtual Teams* by Debbie DuFrene and Carol Lehman
- *Corporate Communication: Tactical Guidelines for Strategic Practice* by Michael Goodman and Peter B. Hirsch
- *Communicating to Lead and Motivate* by William C. Sharbrough
- *Communication Strategies for Today's Managerial Leader* by Deborah Roebuck
- *Communication in Responsible Business: Strategies, Concepts, and Cases* by Roger N. Conaway and Oliver Laasch
- *Web Content: A Writer's Guide* by Janet Mizrahi
- *Intercultural Communication for Managers* by Michael B. Goodman
- *Today's Business Communication: A How-To Guide for the Modern Professional* by Jason L. Snyder and Robert Forbus
- *Fundamentals of Writing for Marketing and Public Relations: A Step-by-Step Guide for Quick and Effective Results* by Janet Mizrahi
- *Managerial Communication: Evaluating the Right Dose* by Johnson J. David
- *Leadership Talk A Discourse Approach to Leader Emergence* by Robyn C. Walker and Yolanta Aritz
- *SPeak Performance: Using the Power of Metaphors to Communicate Vision, Motivate People, and Lead Your Organization to Success* by Jim Walz

FORTHCOMING IN THIS COLLECTION

- *Communication Beyond Boundaries 8/15/2014* by Payal Mehra

Announcing the Business Expert Press Digital Library

*Concise E-books Business Students Need
for Classroom and Research*

This book can also be purchased in an e-book collection by your library as

- a one-time purchase,
- that is owned forever,
- allows for simultaneous readers,
- has no restrictions on printing, and
- can be downloaded as PDFs from within the library community.

Our digital library collections are a great solution to beat the rising cost of textbooks. e-books can be loaded into their course management systems or onto student's e-book readers.

The **Business Expert Press** digital libraries are very affordable, with no obligation to buy in future years. For more information, please visit **www.businessexpertpress.com/librarians**. To set up a trial in the United States, please contact **Adam Chesler** at *adam.chesler@ businessexpertpress.com* for all other regions, contact **Nicole Lee** at *nicole.lee@igroupnet.com*.

CPSIA information can be obtained
at www.ICGtesting.com
Printed in the USA
FFHW010750110919
54844808-60556FF